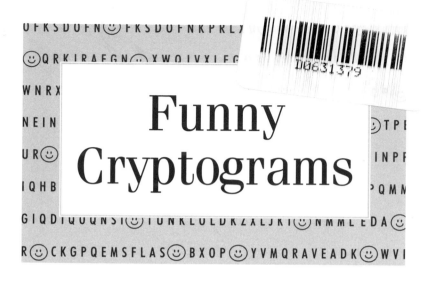

Funny Cryptograms

Shawn Kennedy

STERLING PUBLISHING CO., INC.
New York

To Susan West,
whose creativity and support
have helped transform a hobby into a career.

6   8   10   9   7

Published by Sterling Publishing Co., Inc.
387 Park Avenue South, New York, NY 10016
© 2003 by Shawn Kennedy
Distributed in Canada by Sterling Publishing,
% Canadian Manda Group, 165 Dufferin Street,
Toronto, Ontario, Canada M6K 3H6
Distributed in Great Britain and Europe by Chris Lloyd at Orca Book
Services, Stanley House, Fleets Lane, Poole BH15 3AJ, England
Distributed in Australia by Capricorn Link (Australia) Pty. Ltd.,
P.O. Box 704, Windsor, NSW 2756, Australia

Sterling ISBN 1-4027-0139-X

For information about custom editions, special sales, premium and
corporate purchases, please contact Sterling Special Sales
Department at 800-805-5489 or specialsales@sterlingpub.com.

C☺NTENTS

Introduction
4

Hints
6

Cryptograms
8

Answers
78

INTRODUCTION

Most health experts agree that laughter is therapeutic for the mind, body, and spirit. It's like internal jogging; it increases the heartbeat, brings in oxygen, and stimulates circulation. It allows your body to relax and makes you feel better. Most important, it allows us to maintain a positive attitude when we're faced with all of life's little challenges.

If laughter truly is the best medicine, then consider this book a giant dose of solving fun. This collection of coded quotations is specially designed to give you a good time. All of these knee-slappers will have you grinning, groaning, and laughing until it hurts. The humorous quotations come from a wide range of your favorite celebrities, from comedians Johnny Carson and Dave Barry to Henry Kissinger, Newt Gingrich, and others you never would suspect to have a sense of humor. Decoding each puzzle is like having stand-up comedy wherever your travels may take you.

So sharpen your pencil, roll up your sleeves, and let the solving, and laughter, begin!

HOW TO SOLVE CRYPTOGRAMS

Don't be discouraged by these strings of seemingly meaningless letters. You don't have to be a CIA agent to decode them. In case you are new to this puzzle type, here is a crash course in cryptography.

Each sentence is a coded message. The letters of the original message are called plaintext, and have been replaced by other letters. No letter can represent itself, and substitutions remain consistent throughout each puzzle, but vary from one cryptogram to the next. The text in the puzzle is called the ciphertext.

In the example below, each of the three C's represents a U, the two X's represent O's, and so on.

LAUGHING OUT LOUD

EZCRYPTR XCM EXCQ

Solving cryptograms relies on trial and error, but there are several hints that can help you along the way.

Little words can be big indicators. One-letter words are always A or I, and two-letter words are often prepositions and other "filler" words like OF, OR, IS, AT, TO, etc. The word THAT is easy to spot, since it begins and ends with the same letter. Locating THAT can also reveal where THE might be lurking. Other words to watch for include DID, GOING, NEVER, LITTLE, and PEOPLE.

Work back and forth between short words that share multiple letters. Common similar words include OF and FROM, YOU and YOUR, THE and THEN, THEY and THEIR, and HE and HIS.

Punctuation can tell you a lot about a sentence. If a cryptogram ends with a question mark, the first word is usually an interrogative (such as WHO, WHAT, or WHERE). Words directly outside quotation marks are likely to be synonyms of SAID or SAYS. In addition, a series of words set off by commas indicates that a word toward the end of the series is AND or OR. Watch for apostrophes, which are often followed by S or T.

Scan the ciphertext for any repeated word endings, which are likely to be -ED, -LY, -ING, and -TION. If a certain letter appears mostly at the ends of words, try E or S.

Every word has vowels, and it is sometimes useful to try to pinpoint them in each word.

In two-letter words, one letter must always be a vowel.

Doubled letters in longer words are usually LL, NN, or TT, while doubled letters in the center of shorter words are usually EE and OO.

If a letter appears only once or twice in a cryptogram, then it is probably a consonant. Certain consonants frequently appear together, such as TH, SH, CH, NG, and so on.

Sometimes it is possible to deduce the author of the quotation given only its letter pattern. We've also included letter hints to help you get started on each puzzle. They appear on pages 6 and 7. The first letter is the ciphertext and the letter after the arrow is its plaintext equivalent.

If all else fails, and nobody is looking, the answers are in the back of the book. Peeking at the first word will often help tremendously.

—Shawn Kennedy

HINTS

1. Z → P
2. V → L
3. I → N
4. O → D
5. K → W
6. A → C
7. G → U
8. P → S
9. C → H
10. X → B
11. G → I
12. U → W
13. H → C
14. H → A
15. P → R
16. E → N
17. M → O
18. E → L
19. D → E
20. J → D
21. F → I
22. Q → C
23. I → E
24. Z → D
25. A → R
26. M → P
27. J → T
28. R → N
29. M → H
30. F → W
31. E → L
32. F → O
33. Z → R
34. A → T
35. M → P
36. V → Y
37. F → A
38. N → I
39. Z → U

40. Y → A
41. V → C
42. M → V
43. I → A
44. R → C
45. T → U
46. J → N
47. S → C
48. B → M
49. P → Y
50. S → R
51. S → E
52. W → O
53. B → W
54. G → N
55. X → H
56. X → B
57. Q → M
58. W → G
59. R → F
60. R → V
61. U → L
62. T → C
63. D → P
64. V → I
65. K → M
66. E → W
67. X → T
68. R → B
69. X → U
70. X → W
71. O → G
72. Z → K
73. Z → T
74. V → G
75. T → F
76. N → B
77. G → Y
78. F → W

79. G → O
80. X → G
81. K → V
82. L → M
83. B → O
84. G → L
85. Y → C
86. W → P
87. K → R
88. V → E
89. C → G
90. K → R
91. S → H
92. P → I
93. D → S
94. E → M
95. L → E
96. A → T
97. J → M
98. G → A
99. X → H
100. W → D
101. X → M
102. D → B
103. P → V
104. P → L
105. J → P
106. X → K
107. Y → M
108. T → E
109. X → J
110. W → N
111. L → I
112. G → A
113. N → C
114. F → A
115. D → W
116. O → G
117. X → D

118. E → L
119. D → M
120. C → E
121. I → P
122. W → C
123. G → O
124. V → D
125. H → M
126. Y → R
127. U → W
128. T → S
129. K → O
130. N → Y
131. F → Y
132. S → N
133. S → K
134. K → L
135. N → I
136. P → W
137. L → R
138. W → N
139. D → C
140. B → H
141. B → V
142. T → N
143. V → U
144. R → D
145. H → B
146. J → K
147. U → W
148. B → A
149. P → O
150. V → D
151. U → R
152. S → W
153. H → N
154. R → V
155. T → R
156. J → O

157. P → I
158. C → H
159. H → G
160. U → N
161. L → M
162. Z → E
163. P → O
164. Y → D
165. T → D
166. T → A
167. A → E
168. A → S
169. Q → K
170. L → I
171. M → L
172. T → S
173. L → M
174. V → A
175. D → A
176. K → D
177. R → F
178. F → W
179. Q → D
180. R → N
181. I → D
182. O → A
183. F → P
184. K → T
185. Q → L
186. A → O
187. P → C
188. N → R
189. H → O
190. S → A
191. C → D
192. H → E
193. T → G
194. I → A
195. L → H

196. R → T
197. R → C
198. J → O
199. Y → H
200. Q → P
201. C → U
202. B → M
203. I → E
204. B → E
205. Y → I
206. C → L
207. L → F
208. X → Y
209. L → E
210. R → M
211. N → A
212. P → W
213. Y → M
214. R → O
215. X → T
216. A → P
217. C → U
218. J → P
219. Z → O
220. Z → C
221. E → R
222. S → V
223. R → S
224. J → D
225. L → Y
226. G → A
227. I → W
228. Q → L
229. G → M
230. I → R
231. P → V
232. U → O
233. R → T
234. R → M

235. M → F	258. R → N	281. Z → T	304. B → R	327. M → U	350. A → F
236. N → C	259. B → A	282. C → D	305. G → S	328. D → W	351. I → D
237. Y → E	260. T → Y	283. N → L	306. T → U	329. X → W	352. C → H
238. S → H	261. M → T	284. Q → V	307. T → C	330. I → Y	353. L → H
239. U → T	262. P → R	285. E → P	308. U → L	331. T → Y	354. Z → N
240. A → R	263. C → G	286. Y → P	309. N → S	332. M → W	355. C → K
241. T → U	264. Y → V	287. Y → H	310. O → L	333. Q → F	356. V → P
242. E → T	265. X → P	288. Z → D	311. M → P	334. V → M	357. E → W
243. R → E	266. G → P	289. Y → P	312. A → G	335. Y → L	358. S → W
244. C → O	267. B → I	290. H → F	313. M → U	336. T → P	359. P → M
245. G → N	268. X → W	291. M → L	314. M → W	337. E → L	360. V → L
246. G → H	269. L → C	292. G → S	315. J → U	338. R → U	361. W → G
247. H → F	270. C → G	293. H → M	316. Z → G	339. P → M	362. N → G
248. I → W	271. J → C	294. F → U	317. M → S	340. W → M	363. R → M
249. T → F	272. X → M	295. M → O	318. Z → O	341. O → C	364. Q → F
250. Z → N	273. E → Y	296. K → I	319. C → V	342. X → D	365. P → C
251. L → H	274. Y → D	297. S → L	320. K → C	343. B → K	366. Q → D
252. Z → I	275. X → C	298. N → H	321. V → R	344. Q → L	367. W → M
253. U → L	276. L → E	299. K → G	322. Y → D	345. B → P	368. D → L
254. J → C	277. F → C	300. F → C	323. N → C	346. M → R	369. E → M
255. D → G	278. Z → L	301. Q → U	324. G → C	347. A → R	370. Q → G
256. N → M	279. O → D	302. M → R	325. E → C	348. J → N	
257. K → C	280. M → F	303. V → E	326. X → H	349. C → B	

1. T AKNB EAB ZBLSBHE GTVZFTSTBW EKO SMLV SML EAB QMNBLCVBCE. JAI WMC'E EABI UPGE ZLTCE MPL VMCBI JTEA K LBEPLC KWWLBGG MC TE? —DMD AMZB

2. PET ZRWTUPWJWR PETIHA W VWYT NTZP WZ PEFP PET HWUOZ IJ ZFPSHU FHT RIGLIZTK TUPWHTVA IJ VIZP FWHVWUT VSOOFOT. —GFHY HSZZTVV

3. OVH OTJYRBH SPOV GJUUPIU PN OVWO, RX OVH OPEH XJY THWBPQH XJY'TH IJO PI NVWMH DJT PO, PO'N OJJ DWT OJ SWBF RWLF. —DTWIFBPI M. GJIHN

4. RMEVPGJP VD DHNPEAVGW UHT MONVZP VG EAP OZVKPZ CPAVGO UHT, MGO DJHZG VG EAP HGP MAPMO. —NMJ NJJFPMZU

5. PRLX DJJLBCFERAJ DXN PRLX KEAQRKJ RA FGN KRXWQ. JVXLO FGNB RSS NTNXP RAVN EA D KGEWN, RX FGN WEYGF KRA'F VRBN EA. —DWDA DWQD

8

6. LQFN PFOYVMUE. ZFQ'R SAAMWR PFOY
ZFB'V SZXCYSRCFQ SV AFQAUOVCKM MKCZMQAM
RTSR PFO SYM NFQZMYEOU.   —SQQ USQZMYV

7. BOIM QEM QGLO YXLI BOXYNQ EVPGB
TIPTHI EB BOIXA JGYIAEHQ BOEB XB RESIQ RI
QEW BOEB X'R NPXYN BP RXQQ RXYI VM KGQB E
JIF WEMQ.   —NEAAXQPY SIXHHPA

8. TB'P YUYCTJM BIYB BIO YUAKJB AH JOEP
BIYB IYVVOJP TJ BIO EAWZX ONOWD XYD YZEYDP
FKPB OLYSBZD HTBP BIO JOEPVYVOW.
                              —FOWWD POTJHOZX

9. EUJ'P OJUNO PCQ DQZPCQH; JKJQ-PQJPCI
UM PCQ XQUXRQ NUFREJ'P IPZHP Z
NUJWQHIZPKUJ KM KP EKEJ'P NCZJYQ UJNQ KJ Z
DCKRQ.   —OKJ CFAAZHE

10. STFLJIY NUAO TYG FUODYOC RYL JTLU S
KSX LURYLZYO GJLZUAL SORAJTR, S XSTD
OUXXYOF ZSC WACL LSDYT VMSKY.
                              —WUZTTF KSOCUT

11. DU WNMUMIGKC GK DU WYJWQC BPM BGZZ
XUMB CMIMQQMB BPL CPW CPGUFK PW
JQWHGNCWH LWKCWQHDL HGHU'C PDJJWU.

—WDQZ BGZKMU

12. BRXMV FMQYZ JY XPM VJBN KJ IOAP Q
UBYX XJ KWMYN IJVM XQIM UQXP IE RBIQDE,
UPJ Q PMBV BVM UJYNMVROD WMJWDM.

—PJUQM IBYNMD

13. NJD HMG IJC VR RPSRHARK AJ YJERTG M
HJCGATI ANMA NML ADJ NCGKTRK MGK
BJTAI-LXP QXGKL JB HNRRLR?

—HNMTORL KR YMCOOR

14. ATCI TX ATJI H G-QWMTI. ZWE LWK'V NHKV
VW AIHMI TK VPI QTLLAI WC TV, GEV ZWE LWK'V
NHKV VW XII TV HOHTK. —VIL VEUKIU

15. GA GAPA IS NSSP GA KJE TS KSW GJWAP.
ZRW CW ECET'W QJWWAP ZAUJRIA GA KJE TS
ZJWKWRZ WS NRW CW CT JTMGJM.

—WSQ EPAAIAT

10

16. AUT YBTLYCT KTEFOI OM MTBTE OEFUTM

IQEC, ROAU VSMA Y UYID-OEFU TLYMTL—OE

FYMT ZQS AUQSCUA QKAOXOMX RYM JTYJ.

—LQHTLA HLYSIA

17. DRPP ZPRQOMQ'H KMYGRNQ BMPRZS

GEBGYRGQZG HOGUH UXRQPS KYMU WXLRQN

DYGXTKXHO XO OWG RQOGYQXORMQXP WMAHG MK

BXQZXTGH. —BXO DAZWXQXQ

18. STCHC KTWNEL MC KWYC KBTWWEK BJEECL

LCVWHYJSWHACK SW XTABT UCWUEC JHC KCOS AV

STCZ JHC SWW PWWL SW MC UHJBSABJE.

—KJYNCE MNSECH

19. JU AWZ SC YW YXFR YW UWK, XEB UWKG

AWZ SC YW FSCYDE. SH UWK HSESCO HSGCY,

VFDXCD FDY JD REWM. —OXGGU ODGCOHSDFB

20. SAQ SL BM ZYVQL TQRTQIX JDTVAR BM

MQWTX VA IYQ IYQWIQT VX IYWI V ZSDOJA'I XVI

VA IYQ WDJVQAZQ WAJ HWIZY BQ.

—KSYA EWTTMBSTQ

11

21. F ANVQ QH B YNOQBWYBVQ QGBQ ONYPNO
LYNBJMBOQ BQ BVD QFSN. OH F HYTNYNT
MYNVUG QHBOQ TWYFVX QGN YNVBFOOBVUN.

—OQNPNV AYFXGQ

22. VMND PNRR SFWFZ AF T QNWNRNIFY
QHBSVZU BSVNR PF DOFSY JHZF JHSFU LHZ
AHHXD VMTS PF YH LHZ QMFPNSE EBJ.

—FRAFZV MBAATZY

23. ARYFCG AH ARI BFAIPGAYAI RBLRVYU
GUGAIJ, BA BG FHV DHGGBZEI AH APYOIE XPHJ
THYGA AH THYGA VBARHWA GIIBFL YFUARBFL.

—TRYPEIG CWPYEA

24. ZAZ ENJ VOVT GYQB AD Y TNNU YDZ
CNTSVF GRE ENJ GYQBVZ AD? A FRADB FRYF'H
RNG ZNSH HWVDZ FRVAT QAOVH.   —HJV UJTWRE

25. WUBYN YAB VWSB AYRRWGN. PTE IBG Y
LTEOVB YCU VBYAC QTX GT QYCUVB GQBJ, YCU
OABGGP NTTC PTE QYZB Y UTFBC.

—HTQC NGBWCRBLS

12

26. Z FCPHK'Y LHMGLYHI NA NZBBZKT WLHIZY

WCLI YG YFH MGJZWH QHWCEBH SFGHPHL BYGJH

ZY ZB BMHKIZKT JHBB YFCK NA SZDH.

—ZJZH KCBYCBH

27. BVA TMF NMROSB HAWYN JIN TIMGMTJNG

VP M QMF CB IVL IN JGNMJR JIVRN LIV TMF WV

FVJIOFY PVG IOQ. —HMQNR W. QOSNR

28. OXK DKAO FZC OG BKKW HXLTSQKR XGVK

LA OG VZBK OXK XGVK ZOVGAWXKQK

WTKZAZRO—ZRS TKO OXK ZLQ GIO GY OXK

OLQKA. —SGQGOXC WZQBKQ

29. VMS JMTWAO UDTUAD ET TWZ FHO UFS ZT

JDD NFO KTIBDJ VMDH ZMDS QFH JZFS FZ MTKD

FHO JDD NFO ZDADIBJBTH GTP HTZMBHE?

—JFKWDA ETAOVSH

30. TMGELP T FXYGELP FYEVCY FOTV OC

VOELGM TAXNV HYEVEHM EM ZEGC TMGELP T

ZTIBBXMV OXF EV DCCZM TAXNV QXPM.

—HOYEMVXBOCY OTIBVXL

13

31. S'Z ESYX PT VXX PNX CTAXGKJXKP CXP TWP TU OMG MEPTCXPNXG MKZ EXMAX PNX ONTEX USXEZ PT HGSAMPX SKZWVPGQ.

—RTVXHN NXEEXG

32. RSPQXW, FE GFTKPX, JDP LJX YXPL GDPLSQA. SE JX RFXPQ'L OSVX DQ DGLFK JX PSIHOW LXDKP JSI TH. —DOEKXR JSLGJGFGV

33. F CVTOY OCPL VODCWSZ CXSEW LFV HZOQOZODPOV QSZ WLO HZOVFYODPM, CDY DFDOWM-VFA VODCWSZV OCPL ZOPOFROY SDO RSWO. —BSLD Q. TODDOYM

34. KZBBTR MPR: USRI LQO'GR SQKR QI NMAOGBML IZPSA, ASR ARTRDSQIR GZIPN, MIB LQO SQDR ZA'N ASR UGQIP IOKJRG.

—GZIP TMGBIRG

35. L CILGD YZG BIR IWFZ W MLZTNZJ ZWT WTZ VZCCZT MTZMWTZJ KRT YWTTLWEZ. CIZU'FZ ZPMZTLZGNZJ MWLG WGJ VRHEIC OZBZQTU.

—TLCW THJGZT

14

36. VEI'LR ETNV QRLR JEL U WQELC KDWDC.
SET'C QILLV. SET'C HELLV. UTS ZR WILR CE
WGRNN CQR JNEHRLW UNETF CQR HUV.

—HUNCRL QUFRT

37. QEYYEBOU YBOZ LBK EQQBKXFYEXR SVB MB
OBX HOBS SVFX XB MB SEXV XVJQUJYNJU BO F
KFEOR UDOMFR FLXJKOBBO.   —UDUFO JKXW

38. ND PRJ RCQ PRJL KHUT H VJUSLQS
IRJUSE, PRJ VHBQ H ILRKFQX; KJZ ND PRJ RCQ
PRJL KHUT H XNFFNRU, NZ VHE.

—ARVU XHPUHLS TQPUQE

39. QTJ UNXQJXQ SNC QK XZGGJJL AX QK MKKY
NX AU CKZ NFJ HMNCAWP VC KQTJF HJKHMJ'X
FZMJX, STAMJ EZAJQMC HMNCAWP VC CKZF KSW.

—OAGTNJM YKFLN

40. EFDC FU OBFOEB DIZKG DIBN'MB
LIYMZDYJEB ZU DIBN PZHB YSYN DIBZM FEX
LEFDIBC YKX DIZKPC DIBN XFK'D SYKD.

—VNMDEB MBBX

15

41. ANZXZ'H HM YQVN KJIHAFV FE ANFH

VQJAQXZ ANIA BFESJ JZMKIXP HUFE FH

GZVMYFER IE ZEPIERZXZP HSEANZAFV.

—JFJS AMYJFE

42. LE CDZ QLMX YD YWX ITX DE I WZOSFXS

CDZ WIMX LY GISX VXNIZAX MXFC EXP KXDKQX

SLX KIAY YWX ITX DE I WZOSFXS.

—TXDFTX VZFOA

43. ZIKGUVHV VGACN IXSTH CUCAHQ GAKLACH

SJ HZAUK OUMAV HTCUCW HZAUK ZIKGV ICN HAC

GAKLACH GOIQUCW STH SJ HTCA.

—UWSK VHKIMUCVYQ

44. UYAIKLP ZG CUFUYC L TZVUIURULY INK

HKDA IZ INK RUID, UI QUCNI EK EKIIKX IZ

RNLYCK INK VZRHA.   —PZSC VLXAZY

45. NZCCOYZZA'U M FCMJH YNHVH BNHO'CC

FMO OZT M BNZTUMLA AZCCMVU QZV M PWUU,

MLA QWQBO JHLBU QZV OZTV UZTC.

—EMVWCOL EZLVZH

46. AN VSM XMHMJ GKFPNX, AJTE GAIME SFG F XSFHMJ NFOM. VSDX XSACTG VMTT CX XABMVSDJQ FRACV VSM OCXVAB AN XSFHDJQ.

—VAB PARRDJX

47. U CEHN YNAK PBXNBF KP TN EVEQNRNX EK ERD KUIN UR SEFN PA REKUPREY NINBMNRSD, NHNR UA U'I UR E SETURNK INNKURM.

—BPREYX BNEMER

48. C KROCJIQR YJFD BCX PD RQD KQMORDKR TJKRCFED PDRVDDF RVM SMJFRK, PZR JR JK PX FM BDCFK RQD BMKR JFRDODKRJFI.

—TMERMO VQM

49. X'Y TKLKZVXW KOVGE NHNLPEJXZS. VZ YP MEKEXVZKLP OXIPIQN X JKHN K LNKLHXNC YXLLVL.

—LXIJKLW QNCXM

50. J TIIF DZWKVXVS ZW XIK WIGVIXV NZKP XIKPZXT KI WJU. J TIIF DZWKVXVS ZW J TIIF KJDQVS NZKP J WISV KPSIJK.

—QJKPJSZXV NPZKVPISX

51. ZUYUDAUYO DSWPYV UY FAS PQJXNUWD OSFD JPL DUQISK. ZUYUDAUYO DSWPYV UY NPQUFUWD OSFD JPL PTQUIUPY.

—KUWACKV XUQAPLD YUBPY

52. E FA PWX MEKKEPT XW SECN XOZ KEYZC WR TZSAFP CWKHEZSC RWS BWQPXSEZC MOWCZ PFAZC MZ BFPPWX CDZKK DSWDZSKL.

—YWKNZS SQOZ

53. PRF KGZQFTP BGUJ YZ PRF FZQKYTR KDZQMDQF YT PRF GZF PRDP WGKKGBT PRF NRUDTF, "DZJ ZGB D BGUJ WUGL GMU TNGZTGU."

—RDK FDPGZ

54. LKLG WUAL LFVYOLAVZMGE ZPVG ZPL EQI BPU ZPMGSY PL SGUBY MZ VRR MY ZPL UGL BPU ALVRRI NULY.

—VR CLAGYZLMG

55. J EDMP HEFRXB LQ ZJGC I CPB EY HIBBPUJPC YEU MXUJCBLIC VJBX I DEBP ED JB CIQJDR, "BEQC DEB JDMTFGPG."

—HPUDIUG LIDDJDR

18

56. PWLCFUOH DUO GWO IVTG FOTLUDXCO

VNNVHOHGT DG TPUDXXCO DT GWOA DUO XVGW

ODTA GV XODG DHF RZH GV PWODG.

—RUDH COXVSLGE

57. IZX VAWN SLBV IAX HZUKO BPZ XAWHK'O

JWZUBZOB SLBLZO LI BPZ IDQEZW AT MZAMHZ

UWADIK XPAQ VAD OPADHKI'B QUNZ U ODKKZI

QARZ. —KURLK HZBBZWQUI

58. DAG TU QBKTL LBMW BM HAN JUKMBMW?

BH'L HAN HKBXJSAIMH LAUXH: "DN WUH

HAKUXWA IMUHANK MBWAH." —NMBT QIWMUOT

59. UN UOV VRRZDZPQQS WPQMN RKNNHVL VR

AINNDO PFVWN QZRN ZEANQR ANNL EV OPWN

YVEOZYJ EV EPQC PFVME FME EON UNPEONK.

—FPKFPKP NOKNYKNZDO

60. XKA X QXF PGBSG PXJ GL BK VDBFV ZD

RDZL, XFI GL PBWW TNDCXCWJ ZLWW JDE. XKA

GBQ, GDPLRLN, PGJ, XFI RXVELFLKK BK XWW.

—CLNFXNI WLRBF

19

61. DUKPLVLA GQXW EQXCK MEVUK GQXW SVBC

PWK CZVUU AWQMVLA VC UVSK CEQRKUVLA ZEK

MPUS JKNQWK VZ CZQIC CLQMVLA.

—IEGUUVC BVUUKW

62. E THRXPHRDVY DV QGY EPQ HU CDKDCDZW

E TEFY DZ VITG E AEN QGEQ YKYPNHZY

MYBDYKYV GY GEV QGY MDWWYVQ XDYTY.

—BICADW YPGEPC

63. O'K S DVOZBNBDVG KSTBQ. PVSP KYSIN O

FSI PVOIE WYYD PVBJXVPN SMBJP MYOIX

JIYKDZBGYW.   —MQJFY ZYY

64. VD INWWTCNNJ, ED GUFVLEXWG JVONHKG

MGLLWGAGDL AGEDM GEKI REHLT BGLLVDB

PVPLT RGHKGDL NP LIG RFXWVKVLT.

—WEFHGD XEKEWW

65. PMQJ ECQD MWJ M RQCROQ LQMKO CL

KAWJ RQORMQO ZCN LCQ VPO GNFDZ UQOMDH

VPMV LAWMGGZ FCKO MGCWT—CQ JCW'V.

—PMQQAHCW LCQJ

20

66. W'FJ QVWUJM V RJE ZNTUMC VGNTUM HAJ PWMMKJ. HAJ NUKB KNEJG-ONMB QVGPJUHC W NEU HAVH CHWKK RWH PJ YNPRNGHVOKB VGJ HNEJKC. — MVFJ OVGGB

67. SHIHK AKMP MAJTX ZJTK MSLHYXJKY LJEQSP JIHK JS XCH EMZODJVHK; XCH QEEQPKMXQJS DMVY VHKHS'X MY YXKQLX QS XCJYH NMZY. — DHV DHCK

68. ZF'C CFAIQBN WKY LNY KL FWN YKAUT'C BANIF MAKRUNHC IAN CKUJNT RG MNKMUN YWK ANHNHRNA FWNZA IUBNRAI. — WNARNAF MAKDWQKY

69. IVXC FKPC QKZCA UXJCIFN, EJIOKXI RBWWCVA KV TFBAOJWD FJDOIA. JT NKX OCBV RCFFA, DCI NKXV CBVA QOCQMCY. — CVJQO ACDBF

70. SR DHM CHU'J XBUJ JH XHNA, DHM GBKV JH XHNA JH VBNU VUHMFG EHUVD OH JGBJ DHM XHU'J GBKV JH XHNA. — HFCVU UBOG

21

71. NWZONAZUNJA NM Z OJJV LJPMG UJ KZPPH

HJR JSGP ULG OPJRAV—AJU Z DCHNAO KZPXGU

UJ MGU HJR DPGG DPJW XPJTZTNCNUH.

—PJTGPUMJA VZSNGM

72. JEQBDP JFO JBTJWP JPZGHX BGDDBO ZGEP

TKJD DKOW TJHD DL NO TKOH DKOW XFLT QV—

'AJQPO DKOW'FO BLLZGHX MLF GEOJP.

—VJQBJ VLQHEPDLHO

73. L ZETUQCZ QC L XBRREY YNE IUQABC

ZNETCLPIC EX FQRBC CE NB JLP WB

GNEZEOULGNBI CZLPIQPO QP XUEPZ EX NQC

JLU. —BFQRB OLPBCZ

74. REI'J RJ EJGKIVC? JFC EKTC OCXOHC MFX

HKAVF KJ VWOEW BXGJAIC JCHHCGE JKDC

CQXIXTREJE ECGRXAEHW.

—QRIQRIIKJR CIYARGCG

75. HSZXSB ANX KHZK IJKGSBKKUBS YBHC GS

THLOK, SXO TGLOGXS, NHK SBMBQ QBHY XCY

TGMB-ZBHQ VQXDBLOGXSK. —UHCLXCU TXQIBK

22

76. Q'K FQSJP VM WGG FLQY DVDYJDYJ WNVTF

NJWTFI NJQDZ VDGI YEQD PJJH. FLWF'Y PJJH

JDVTZL. XLWF PV IVT XWDF, WD WPVSWNGJ

HWDRSJWY?   —BJWD EJSS

77. SXNJHPG JWLOSWN RN JSLJ DWU LUY

ULJXHUN TWSLCW FXNWBG HUOW JSWG SLCW

WQSLRNJWY LBB HJSWP LBJWPULJXCWN.

                                             —LTTL WTLU

78. VGZD ELZ IPXQU EFED FXVG ILXMZ-XQB.

QPF FGZLZ ELZ VGZ VZZQEUZLB UPXQU VP UP VP

QPV FEVNG E RPMXZ?   —TPT VGPREB

79. GZIV GZH FHYNGZ SZ O RUGLNOZP SN O

QGYH, OZP UH SN SZRHYHNRSZJ QHMOLNH UH

SN GZH FHYNGZ SZ O RUGLNOZP.

                                             —UOYGIP ZSMGINGZ

80. KRSP HP HDI SCPM CV VGMYW WIOCYX WH

PCYF VHLMWKCYX WH FH UCWK WKM WCLM UM

KRQM IDVKMF WKIHDXK SCPM WIOCYX WH VRQM.

                                             —UCSS IHXMIV

23

81. ~~The advantage of having a bad memory~~
X Z Y   C F K C H X C S Y   E O   Z C K Q H S   C   A C F   V Y V E I U
~~is that several times over one enjoys~~
Q N   X Z C X ,   N Y K Y I C W   X Q V Y N   E K Y I ,   E H Y   Y H G E U N
~~the same good things for the first time~~
X Z Y   N C V Y   S E E F   X Z Q H S N   O E I   X Z Y   O Q I N X   X Q V Y .

~~friedrick Nietzsche~~
—O I Q Y F I Q J Z   H Q Y X D N J Z Y

82. J M U X ,   A J   K J B   L U B H   L U I   V Q E A S ,   W Y S

B J H A I ' S   H R H E X J I H   L U M H   U   E J Y K G   B E U V S   W H V J E H

S G H X   L U M H   U   L U A S H E N Q H F H ?   —F J Y E S I H X   G Y A S J I

83. Q P   K E K A K N O   D X T G B E T X   I N T   A B   T S X   W X D

Z B D   H X Z N Q N A K B E   B Z   U W N D N U A X D ,   Y S A   A W X E   K

D X N O K R X H   A W N A   K   W N H   E B   U W N D N U A X D .

—U W N D O X T   Y N D V O X P

84. C V X G V Y W   D O V T V T   V T   M B U M   C Z C W I M   P B W I

Q Z S   O W U G V F W   Q Z S O   D B V G X O W I   U I X   Q Z S O

D G Z M B W T   U O W   U K Z S M   M B W   T U C W   U N W .

—K V G G   M U C C W S T

85. Y H R T M B U Q D   P W N N   K U C U Q   Q U T N J Y U   B E U

P J D B U L J D O U B   P E U K   W B   Y H R U D   B H

D B Q U J R N W K W K Z   H S S W Y U   P H Q O .

—Y N J V B H K   U N P U N N

24

86. ECYOY SD HKECSHA XKOY XSDYOBZRY SH ECY FKORP ECBH EK BOOSNY SH WBOBPSDY BHP RKKQ RSQY UKVO WBDDWKOE WCKEK.

—YOXB ZKXZYGQ

87. VMJ VKTOAZJ ISVM WTYV TP OY SY VMNV IJ ITOZR KNVMJK AJ KOSFJR AL DKNSYJ VMNF YNQJR AL UKSVSUSYW.

—FTKWNF QSFUJFV DJNZJ

88. UPTMEVS LGUZ OP MEV EXQUP DEUSUDMVS OH MEUM VIVSKWTFK ZUPMH MT WXOGF UPF PTWTFK ZUPMH MT FT QUOPMVPUPDV.

—JXSM ITPPVAXM

89. MEB JBLXBNNPTC MEPTC WYSRM MBTTPN PN MEWM TS AWMMBX ESF CSSJ P CBM, P'DD TBZBX YB WN CSSJ WN W FWDD.

—APMUE EBJYBXC

90. YA TDV JZB KABXKJ BNA DPPAFBHZJ ZP BNZLA YNZ CHEA XL, OXB YA DCYDVL KALUAFB BNAHK QZZI WXIQTAJB.   —CHOOHA PXIHT

91. CSDB ASMZQV HZC DJHLPICLME VICDA ME

RQMCSDA AM TD TMZQV YEMT TSDE CSDB KM MZC

MN ACBQD. —KIPPB ASIEVQLEK

92. P GSIY YD T BPRB XABDDC YBTY GTX XD

MTIRSFDJX, YBS XABDDC ISGXWTWSF BTM TI

DOPYJTFQ ADCJVI. —FDANQ FTQ

93. DPWH-FXDMXKWXEP XD BYPE VAGT

MAEDMXPEMP QPWWD VAG QA FA DASPQYXEJ REF

VAG FAE'Q QRWL ZRML. —B.L. YAKP

94. EYNNHF LTF YW QCF LUMULJN VFJYKN

UCFZ PLQCFJ QYEF WQLJQW XLQXCYZT OV UYQC

EKQCFJ ZLQOJF. —CLJKHN XKPPYZ

95. KFECJ KX UMLC JEB GBJ Q XBKA UKAM AUE

ZQKFX EV ZQCAX, QCI AMLC GBFC Q MEPL KC

AML DEQA. —PQBFLCDL ZLALF

96. V GWHAWU'N USEDAVALWJ LN FVGS RT AYS

JDFRSU WQ SFLJSJA FSJ KYW GLS DJGSU YLN

HVUS. —CSWÚCS RSUJVUG NYVK

26

97. A PADVYF UZFT JL ZVKHQTE WBJFK ZBJF

PYBJ UBYO, AP CZF OAEK QYF KCASS QSAMF,

CZFT A'MF EBTF JL RBH.   —YBKFQTTF

98. TIY DGL JT ATTV TXJ MTO YIBFIYYOL—

JDYN PYBFI RFJD LYRFIB CGQDFIYL GIK YIK XH

RFJD JDY GJTCFQ PTCP.   —CGOQYA HGBITA

99. EB E MRRAEDRU, W ZEB LNUR NK EA

EAEUQXWBM, OCM ANZ W ZEAM VRNVYR MN

MXUWTR EAP OR XEULNAWNCB.   —AWQNYEB QEDR

100. LI WZNC, X EZYZC CZNVXUZW TING N

GZCCXFVZ VLG LQ ZRSVNXEXEA LEZ INK GL WL

XE N HMCWZC!   —NANGIN BICXKGXZ

101. T KILPAIO NR CMN NWI NRTKIN FILN

ORYA. TN XLJIF SRM KRRJ KTJI L YLPX, BLPTAZ,

FIAFTNTQI WMXLA GITAZ.   —PLKCW ARGKI

102. BMJBWH DP VQYP SC SLCHP WCIVFPX SLBV

WCI, DPYBIHP SLPW BXP SLP CVPH JLC JQMM DP

JXQSQVF BDCIS WCI.   —YWXQM YCVVCMMW

27

103. W OWYMKH PWBWFMQG MR QGA JXACA HQZ WCCMPA JMFX OMPA EWVR, OQZC DMIR WGI RAPAG M-FXQZVXF-HQZ-TWBDAI-MFR.

—MPACG EWKK

104. HKO ISJCH CSLW GI NYHBJSHQ SC HKO TSCDGUOJQ HKYH HKO UGPBNO AWGE YPCG HBJWC HG HKO POIH.

—DKSDYLG HJSEBWO

105. MWS BNC'G NPUNME IW XM VTJVAG WJKCKWC. N GSAZVM, KH MWS NEZ N GSAZVM, ERWSPL XV EGSHHVL UKGR IANEERWJJVAE, IAKG NCL UWAOE.

—NCWCMOWSE

106. LYCCKYJS KG QKXS DAKCQKPJ Y IYDVP, DZCPKPJ FYPOGMCKPJG, VC SYDKPJ BFVMGDKBXG. KD QVVXG SYGR ZPDKQ RVZ DCR KD.

—FSQSP CVAQYPO

107. TWKI XPN FKCJW GPF LWK ZLCFZ, XPN YCX IPL ONRLK QKL PIK, ANL XPN TPI'L JPYK NB TRLW C WCISGNM PG YNS KRLWKF.

—MKP ANFIKLL

28

108. D ZBCT MF D LDP ENB FUTPVF FB LXIN

AMLT ADWSMPJ DZBXA NMLFTWG ANDA OBX

IDP'A ADWS DZBXA OBXCFTWG.

—LTWQMWWT WDPVBP

109. QAPP HWZ JZEJPZ AG HWZ BWZUJZT FZUHF

BPUJ DERT WUGSF? UPP HWZ TZFH EO DER, AO

DER'PP XRFH TUHHPZ DERT XZQZPTD.

—XEWG PZGGEG

110. P OLSTQLO P'X MUQPW MJ KUZXPWQ Z

ESUR MJ VLZHUVEUZKU, MTO OLUW P OLSTQLO,

DLJ VLSTYX P? LU WUNUK KUZXV ZWJ SC RPWU.

—VEPHU RTYYPQZW

111. WZS NTVSG L YGNM, WZS TSHH LJFNGWCUW

WZS ONJJC QSONJSH. TSW WZS GSCVSG OCWOZ

ZLH NMU QGSCWZ.

—STLICQSWZ OTCGPHNU IMCGW

112. PMLOKTLOP KNO ROPK ZGI KM BMDYTDBO

PMLOMDO NO TP ZFMDW TP KM AOK NTL NGYO

NTP ZGI.

—FOS M'SMDDOAA

29

113. CVNAVME VF XVRO B FYVUOP'F JOK, BAABNQOU OLOP FM FXVIQAXH YOPQBYF, KZA FAVXX BAABNQOU AM XVCO BA BXX CMZP NMPEOPF. —LVPIVEVB JMMXC

114. P UCNIZ LC TIA ECBV WPLE RCB UE GIFHLG. P'U SFBFTCPZ FTZ TIA ECBV AFX LGI CTHE SHFWI AGIBI UE RIFBX AIBI QDXLPRPIZ. —FTPLF AIPXX

115. SUE VYIYH GYY P NPV DPRBZVM QUDV CAY GCHYYC DZCA P DUNPV DAU APG P RZCCRY WUCLYRRS PVQ P LPRQ GWUC. —YRPSVY LUUGRYH

116. QS KRPOMLTB GVJRZ PN MR ATXIZ XVR QS IGEKQTERB GKZ P UTIZ MPQ TN ATXBVR MR ATXIZ, VT ITKO GV MR ZPZK'U UGJR PU TXU TN QS OGBZRK. —RBPA QTBRAGQLR

117. ULM MB UZH ZYAXHJU LMAXJ SF UZH HFRKSJZ KYFRGYRH UM AZCNH YAH KSBH YFX KMWH—MB YKK LMAXJ. —JUHDZHF JMFXZHSN

30

118. S R C M C Z C A   L   R C D A   D M G B M C   D A W H L M W   O B A

I E D Z C A G,   L   O C C E   D   I J A B M W   L U N H E I C   J B   I C C   L J

J A L C F   B M   R L U   N C A I B M D E E G.

—D K A D R D U   E L M V B E M

119. M T K   W K N A   F N G Q K W   V H   G P M   M T N M

I P D R S M K W H   Z V A A   U K Q V G   M P   M T V G X   A V X K   D K G,

U S M   M T N M   D K G   Z V A A   U K Q V G   M P   M T V G X   A V X K

I P D R S M K W H.

—H E F G K E   T N W W V H

120. H M E J   N F   N X J M C Y   Z C A V C P C S   E Z X D J

Q X X B V K O   V I   J M E J   V L   F X D   H X Y B C S   M E Y S   E K S

G Y X I G C Y C S,   I X N C X K C   C A I C   H X D A S   S X   V J   L X Y

F X D.

—K X Y E   C G M Y X K

121. B R T   U Y T V   M Y O   U T I T M U   Q I Y M   X T B S V,   N Q O

Q I Y M   O T C I T S B C T M O   B M U   W T B A O W.   V Y C T   C T M   B S T

N Y S M   Y A U,   B M U   V Y C T   M T H T S   R S Y P   V Y.

—O S X Y M   T U P B S U V

122. R   K C W P C T   W R E   U S T L   O J F   V J F P R Y M F,   U S P

R E   R T W O J P M W P   W R E   C E B L   R K Q J F M   O J F   W B J M E P

P C   Z B R E P   Q J E M F.

—H T R E Y   B B C L K   N T J I O P

31

123. CM NPF JGCDJ PSS NOGDJ PM RH ZGSSVJV CDMVOTCVN IDMCS C DGDZLPSPDMSH PFYVE, "EG HGI DVVE PDH SPOJV EGDPMCGDF AGO DVN KICSECDJF?"

— MGEE PDEVOFGD

124. QE QF FRXVGA ECNE GOR MNUEF GO TGGV ERUAF, IRLNKFR QZ GOR PRUR GO TGGV ERUAF GOR PGKXV OGE MNUE.

— ANULRX MUGKFE

125. HK UMLPMJ DEYW HW ROB HMCPGR PM AOYW, QVP XGWC O LMVAUC'P NEK PGW QOAA GW DEYW HW ROB HMCPGR HMJW.

— XEAPWJ HEPPGEV

126. PZFYF'N IXF PZBXM OTIDP QZBVSYFX—PZFE XFAFY MI OYIDXS NZIJBXM NXOHNZIPN IW PZFBY MYOXSHOYFXPN.

— TFNNBF & TFDVOZ

127. WHSW RO WZA LHLA HXRCRWM WP EAAD ORCAVW UZRCA WUP YLRAVKO HLA HLIGRVI, HVK MPG EVPU XPWZ PY WZAB HLA ULPVI.

— ZGIZ HCCAV

128. UGVMCMTC MT D RNSSQKAX KQDCS UK

CMWB VNDV SWDLXST D VSDHSVVXS VU TMWY

VNUAYN MW NUV JDVSQ AG VU MVT WUTS.

—NDQUXB NSXKSQ

129. FDFM KDFBVFQYXI URIA QMAIQMUIQDFCO

TMKV IXF URBNQMRC BHCF: VXFM LRI, RBBRMYF

OKHBAFCL QM ACQG ZKAFA.　　　—EKXM VFQIJ

130. LUWWUP OZPOZ MO VYZ WUOV ZBZPHN

IMOVJMAXVZI TXGPVMVN MP VYZ EUJHI.

ZBZJNUPZ VYMPQO YZ YGO ZPUXCY.

—JZPZ IZOLGJVZO

131. QTC RSXWQ QSNC S UCVQ QM BV BNCXSABV

XCWQBGXBVQ, QTCF BWZCY, "TMU NBVF BXC SV

FMGX DBXQF?" S WBSY, "QUM NSHHSMV."

—FBZMP WNSXVMRR

132. X ATFH SEPXKHL PATP PAH NHENGH ZAE

TUH GTPH TUH EMPHS YE WJKA QEGGXHU PATS

PAH NHENGH ZAE ATFH PE ZTXP MEU PAHW.

—H.F. GJKTY

33

133. LIRJNAEANU AD JGGYOAZF YZRDRGK NY XJSR XADNJSRD. JIN AD SZYOAZF OCALC YZRD NY SRRW. —DLYNN JQJXD

134. MUTLJUO WIEJ I UIUJ QFMJU PFL STEJP LF IPGFPJ JKOJ; MJ VIP HFUJ QJFQKJ KFPS IDLJU MJ IUJ BJIB. —OTPVKITU KJMTO

135. TNVIL N'GL KLIRSL X ILVBEXQ KXVJLE, N'GL QLXEVLW BR SASKQL HNBO ZELXB IROLELVIL. —XQXV ZELLVTYXV

136. HFZHVF PRZ ROAF UZ PFONUFQQFQ OKF MFKKCEVF; MRFKF CQ UZ POD ZG MONCUS OIAOUMOSF ZG MRFW. —OUOMZVF GKOUXF

137. VWN LNSCPR JPCV ENPEHN EHSX IPHO MC VP TNSL ZHPVWNC VWNX TPFHU RPV DN ZSFIWV UNSU MR PVWNLTMCN. —LPINL CMJPR

138. OIBX BX V QCSS ZEMWOCG. QEPJX IVTS V CBKIO OE XSWF YS PSOOSCX, VWF B IVTS V CBKIO WEO OE CSVF OISY. —HBPPBVY QVMPJWSC

34

139. CSP RPZ CJ PKPEZCSAGH AV LNCAPGDP.

ZJI HPC CSP DSADRPG QZ SNCDSAGH CSP PHH,

GJC QZ VYNVSAGH AC. —NEGJXM S. HXNVJO

140. NEQZA DBQY GCJ ZSQ ZYLSG ZYH GCJ DTKK

UZAQ MBQ VQNM NEQQFB GCJ DTKK QIQS

SQLSQM. —ZUVSCNQ VTQSFQ

141. WSNU GEQ XEBU RP GUERSRA. PJ UBUR

DPJMU, SI GEQ XEBU E GUERSRA PN DXSHX S

VSMEKKJPBU. —EMXWUSAX FJSWWSERI

142. GQOT BOHBWO PJE LO DA D QPYO PTX

JBPSO FQPTRO, D KOWW KQOL D QPYO DK PK

QHLO DT LX JBPSO GPWWOK. —TDFE PSTOKKO

143. D'AA ODFC KPV GJ DSCG PX ETGM ZDJS PX

OVK TC EGR. RGDJM XUGJYDR EPVAS TGFC

QVJYTCS TDN DJ MTC NPVMT. —OCJC QCUUCM

144. DH ZED PTFF ZEVO E SXOEQ FOEROX PMH

PEDQB QH RH TQ EFF MTZBOFC HX SOQ EFF QMO

UXORTQ CHX RHTDS TQ. —EDRXOP UEXDOSTO

35

145. JYN DFFQM G'LF HFFB ZFAAGBT VGX BYZ ZY HWI SBIZVGBT JYN XI HGNZVKSI, SBK VF MZGAA JYNTYZ ZY HNGBT XF MYXFZVGBT.

—ZSBIS BYF

146. VYR E ZEJR-VA SEPTR GKSC RHRUISCKQD XTNYR ES CEQL EQL LNQ'S UVYC; NSCRUGKYR INV'TT TNNJ TKJR E AESXCGNUJ FVKTS.

—TVXKTTR PETT

147. YGQ KGPL QLBKGO, B VGH GY MGVVAUGGW ZCT KMGHK BQL FIQCGIK HG KLL MGU HMLA'W ZL WQBUO UCHM ZIVTCOT LALK BOW OG FMCO.

—PBHH TQGLOCOT

148. RZVKV BKV FY DFFYWVFR XQARBFPVKA. NZBR NVKV RZVQ PYDFE RZVKV DF RZV UDKAR CGBWV? —NDGGDBO A. XTKKYTEZA

149. N DNHK SKIUI DEH E WMPQ PM SKI SB SP STUM TX SKI NMSIRRNZIMVI. SKIUI'H E WMPQ VERRIG "QUNZKSMIHH," QTS NS GPIHM'S DPUW.

—ZERREZKIU

36

150. CBADT J FWZJD AX J SBPPACIG VAMMARNIS SPJVB, XADRB AS RWDXAXSX QPADRAQJIIG WM VBJIADT FASO ZBD. —KWXBQO RWDPJV

151. R HMB ZYRQVYJ R SMG CXHYTXZG, IYUJYWYUREQY, REH ZM ZDUE RUMDEH ZVUYY ZXNYJ SYCMUY TGXEB HMLE.

—UMSYUZ SYEQVTYG

152. AJ SKHTGDQ VFGRBVINNJ PGQBR BKIHZ F MFJ, JKI UFJ PCPDRIFNNJ QPR RK AP F AKZZ FDM SKHT RSPNCP BKIHZ F MFJ.

—HKAPHR VHKZR

153. NXC TCAETUCT RECG HEN SHRCTGNQHR NXQN JCEJMC BESMR TQNXCT PC BTEHV QHR KEUAETNQPMC NXQH TOVXN OH FQOM.

—AOHMCW JCNCT RSHHC

154. LHLC ZMRXMWXH NDRX LW EZUFW FZTJW, DMX DE WJX TUXLWXFW NLGDU-FLRZMT CLYJZMXF WJX SDUNH XRXU FLS.

—BDFJ GZNNZMTF

155. YSRTR XTR CVTR CRG YSXG PVCRG AG

CRGYXM SVZLAYXMZ—PSAES IWZY DVRZ YV ZSVP

PSV'Z QTAFAGD PSV ETXOH.　　　—LRYRT FRXMR

156. CSM OMQFFR KOVDSCMZVZD CSVZD QYJNC

TVBBFM QDM VG CSM EZJHFMBDM CSQC RJN'FF

DOJH JNC JK VC.　　　—BJOVG BQR

157. QR QCUPAG WBA EVA OPDJ EVAR GVCS PD

MBPGCDG WDJ CD WPBMIWDAG KALWNGA DCKCJR

LWD IAWUA.　　　—KNBE BARDCIJG

158. JBGYBWBGULPB KY RCB CUGI XFGA EFV IF

UNRBG EFV HBR RKGBI FN IFKLH RCB CUGI XFGI

EFV UQGBUIE IKI.　　　—LBXR HKLHGKPC

159. RMW SWDQZL HSDLXCDSWLRQ DLX

HSDLXBMNUXSWL HWR DUZLH QZ YWUU NQ RMDR

RMWF MDKW D BZEEZL WLWEF. —QDE UWKWLQZL

160. ZLV'GY MLN NL WY GYDZ BSDYXVC OX ZLV

HLU'N AULR RFYDY ZLV'DY MLOUM, WYBSVTY

ZLV POMFN ULN MYN NFYDY.　　　—ZLMO WYDDS

161. UW RQTRBY DG U LUW VZF ZUG LUJR UNN YZR LDGYUXRG VZDPZ PUW HR LUJR DW U ORBS WUBBFV ADRNJ. —WDRNG HFZB

162. T DOBZ O SXU XP DXJZF, NQU T GXJ'U VOJU UX UOSB ONXQU UWOU. T VXYB MZYF WOYG OJG T'D VXYUW ZMZYF AZJU. —JOXDT AODKNZSS

163. GM NESY HYAYI CEYR FQPXW JYI FDY. RJY KXRW WYCCR YAYIMPHY RJY'R FR PCL FR E FG. WJYH RJY CEYR FQPXW GM FDY. —IPQYIW PIQYH

164. EOB GBACWY YJQ CL J YDBE DG JMZJQG BJGDBI EOJW EOB LDIGE. SQ EOB GBACWY YJQ QCT'IB CLL DE. —XJAFDB VMBJGCW

165. FK'P TFPUXNVGMFHM KX KQFHI QXE ZGHA OYXODY GVY PQXUIYT LA QXHYPKA, GHT QXE JYE LA TYUYFK. —HXYD UXEGVT

166. KED KFHPISD RQKE SQJQMY SQLD QM KED LTXK STMD QX KETK ZHP YDK KH KED HKEDF DMW QM TM TRLPS EPFFZ. —NHEM NDMXDM

39

167. BE BCDVFQ MVF IWABRI BPFCD VYI FME PFFRI YI BUTFID BI PBO BI B TFDVAQ MVF DBURI BPFCD VAQ FME JVYUOQAE.

—PAEGBTYE OYIQBAUY

168. LA P QAQLRRX TF ENZB P ELBV VF UZV CPT FJ AFGZFBZ ENFAZ KFBHZCALVPFB SFCZA GZ, P WCZVZBT VF LUCZZ.

—LRSZCV KLGQA

169. ZXZ-SXXQH DTFZQ FD'H HFPPV DX FZAJHD DIX TXRCH' IXCQ FZ DIX KFZRDJH' JZMXVKJZD; GRD FY SXXQFZW FH JAOZJHSJZD, HX FH DTJ GOPPJD.

—MRPFO STFPL

170. FBA IAZF SANZEHA PQ N SNT'Z BPTAZFJ LZT'F BLZ LTDPSA FNM HAFEHT. LF'Z FBA YAHP NUCEZF PT BLZ INFBHPPS ZDNGA.

—NHFBEH D. DGNHXA

171. MLDR NKFNTONDHN EYI ZYJREZ XN ZEYZ OD NDRMYDS DLCLSU RLNI ZL ZEN ZENYZNT JDMNII EN LT IEN EYI CTLDHEOZOI.

—GYXNI YRYZN

172. DMYPW JNMTYKMPL YT QYHM NXPPYPW F

EMUMLMNV; VAX'ZM WAL F QAL AI JMAJQM

XPKMN VAX FPK PADAKV'T QYTLMPYPW.

—DYQQ EQYPLAP

173. FDBE NXE QWGV XRWLXGN JRGE XFFXTA

QDBR FDBE'MB TJMRBMBV. W NKCCJNB FDXF'N

QDE LE PJGVHWND QXN NJ TXGL QDBR W

HGKNDBV DWL. —QWGG PWGGBNCWB

174. GAVPIRIN GLJIB JXMP FL PAIK JXMP FL

PGDHI VM GIZZ VM JIB PL WI PALXTAP AVZC VM

TLLF. ZXHODZK, PADM DM BLP FDCCDHXZP.

—HAVNZLPPI GADPPLB

175. K AUWFGI TWJ JDGO AW NFHU DVWFJ

NRAMGB KB JUMSM XMSM DTRVWIR MGAM XUWN

K OTMX DA XMGG. —UMTSR IDZKI JUWSMDF

176. AWF AWOMQ TOAW SDFAFMKOMQ XJI'DF OM

Y QJJK UJJK OH AWYA HJUFAOUFH XJI RYM

YRAIYNNX ADORV XJIDHFNC OMAJ CFFNOMQ

EFAAFD. —RWYDNFH KF NOMA

41

177. G MV QLNLHVGOLQ VZ BEGTQHLO JL
JHAICEN ID GO NELGH RMNELH'F HLTGCGAO, GR
NELZ BMO RGOQ AIN SEMN GN GF.

—BEMHTLF TMVJ

178. FUNM SJ YTH CNHBYHJY YTSPC SP YTH
FUNIK. JU FH JTUQIK JBEH JUWH UZ SY ZUN
YUWUNNUF. —KUP THNUIK

179. R SZH CE Z QZDL YLTLEDIU, ZEQ DBL MWU
DCCA FL BCYHLGZTA YRQREM. DBZD SZH AREQ CX
XWE, WEDRI SL YZE CWD CX VWZYDLYH.

—HWHRL ICWTAH

180. T OMXLPLNI TPPLPKEI JLSS RMP XMSNI
TSS CMKB OBMYSIVX, YKP LP JLSS TRRMC
IRMKZF OIMOSI PM VTAI LP JMBPF PFI IGGMBP.

—FIBV TSYBLZFP

181. ZDX VTZMFHZX OJHT JL ZDX XIVQHZMJKHT
GCGZXF MG ZJ GDMLZ ZJ ZDX MKIMWMIVHT ZDX
NVAIXK JL UVAGVMKO DMG XIVQHZMJK.

—PJDK OHAIKXA

182. YJTA BJTE XOGG BJT SZGG LA BJT CTAOBT, BJT CTAOBZSC WZ AZB IAZY YJTBJTS BZ OACYTS "KSTCTAB" ZS "AZB VQLGBE."

—BJTZWZST SZZCTRTGB

183. FCRFRIMB INSFYNGNMB HPD GRCS: ERK SLWE SRAMX BNB XRL SPQM YPIH XMPC? SPNY NH NA.

—IHPAHRA BMYPFYPAM

184. M'X HCC MT DHBJQ JD WRRNMTL YHTLRQJEV ARHNJTV JEK JD KZR ZHTYV JD DJJCV. CRK'V VKHQK AMKZ KPNRAQMKRQV.

—VJCJXJT VZJQK

185. E SKEQLSA OEQK ERVQL HUMK TUDGVOKG KETS AKEM UDK EDR E SEQY LZOKG SZG UXD XKZFSL ZD ULSKM NKUNQK'G NELZKDTK.

—PUSD VNRZCK

186. VSVZF IWB PWK W ZOTPQ QA DQQVZ XPWQ PV QPOBJK QZDQP, WBR VSVZF AQPVZ IWB PWK W ZOTPQ QA JBAEJ POI RAXB GAZ OQ.

—KWIDVY MAPBKAB

43

187. EGN TYEYON, RPPFOUSHQ EF VFZN VPSNHESVEV, LSAA IN NDRPEAX ASBN EGN JRVE, FHAX TRO ZFON NDJNHVSMN.

—KFGH EGFZRV VARUNB

188. MRX NXOLVS IRK LV JXI WVVA PVVFL ONX INHMMXS HL MROM LV JXI CXVCYX IRV EOS INHMX FSVI OSKMRHSW. —IOYMXN POWXRVM

189. WL AHI PQFX AHIY BJWGSYKF XH WRMYHEK, GKX XJKR HEKYJKQY XJK FWBK XJWFDU AHI UQA QTHIX XJKR XH HXJKYU.

—JQWR DWFHXX

190. EOWOA KFAAT SZFJQ QPO HXNO FL TFJA VPAXHQCSH QAOO. XE QPO OTOH FL VPXIBAOE, QPOT SAO SII QPXAQT LOOQ QSII.

—ISAAT KXIBO

191. DJIGZ UZC LURF DNHH CJ UF RMGB OHGUFG, UZC IGZ UZC CJAF FMJQHC VGHUY UZC AGR QFGC RJ RMG NCGU.

—VJKGVR U. MGNZHGNZ

44

192. WZU VMH OK ZOGH V CZVBH TZFOBM
LQDWAMQ V KLWDI. WBXH FWA'DH VEWVDU,
LQHDH'K BWLQOBM FWA XVB UW VEWAL OL.

—MWZUV IHOD

193. NJDCDNDPB, YDSR JUDL, PQXKYO HR
TRLCYR RLXKTQ CX LXKJDPQ U BUL'P TJXECQ
EDCQXKC ORPCJXADLT QDP JXXCP.

—WJULS U. NYUJS

194. HCREXVZVPA FK I YIA VG VMPIXFUFXP HEC
BXFJCMKC KV HEIH NIX LVCKX'H EIJC HV
CODCMFCXRC FH. —NIO GMFKRE

195. OKMMVXF DVUX WXKELXJ SBX VBPKDZKCDX
DXJJSB: WS WLVBH SU WLVBAJ UKM XBSZAL
KLXKF BSW WS JKR WLXO.

—IXUUXMJSB OKELKOXM

196. EH TDMW TDQ BTXMS RQMM RNXQ MTLQ
HNTP HFMCQ MTLQ FC TDQ BFD RQMM
PXCVNTTPC HNTP RTFSCRTTMC.

—GFRVFNEDQ PFDCHEQMS

45

197. N I R M Q T W T F U R E W   H O T F O I C C   M E C   S I O I W Z

H O T P U V I V   J C   D U N M   S T O I   I B B U R U I Q N   S I E Q C   B T O

F T U Q F   L E R Y D E O V C.   — E W V T J C   M J K W I Z

198. M P J A V Y M   J X F   V W   X V N B   Z B V Y M

V Y S P B O W V Y M X C   K B Y O X V D B F   L J P   O   S P V U B   C J E

G O Q B Y ' I   S J U U V I I B F.   — O Y I G J Y C   K J A B X X

199. W P   G W P U   L U E U   A M J B,   L U   L V M G Z   C U   C V E F

V G Z   X F Z   X R Y W U S U   K V M B Y   X C V M B   B Y U   B W I U   L U ' Z

J X S U Z   U F V M O Y   B V   U F A V K   W B.   — A W I   P W U C W O

200. U S I V K S V   K W K U X K C U X U V E   O U V Z L G V

H L S I V K S V   Q J A I A S H A   U I   Q J L C K C X E   V Z A   C A I V   J L X A

K   F L V Z A J   H K S   Q X K E.   — X L V V A   C K U X E S

201. S O P X Z M   E P O   E C J E Z O :   P O   X I Z V   F R A O Y

Y C G G O Y Y   D P O I   P O   Y E W G A Y   P W Y   I O G A   X C E.

— H R F O Y   S J V R I E   G X I R I E

202. B F T   P Z Q I   T Z L   V R W Q   O D   K Z J P I   F V Z T Q,

P Q I X R L Q   L G Q   E F M L   L G F L   I Z B Q L R B Q I   G Q   G F I   L Z

Q F L   L G Q B.   — F P V F R   I L Q W Q T I Z T

46

203. ZCVGDGFGLJM BEC FCRZVLGJ LOCKD DEI RIPGL LHI VGSI MLGVCHM BEC FCRZVLGJ LOCKD DEI MIL.

—IJCFE ZCBIVV

204. D VX YLP V SBRBPVNDVY FBEVWOB D QLSB VYDXVQO; D VX V SBRBPVNDVY FBEVWOB D GVPB UQVYPO.

—V. AGDPYBC FNLAY

205. LKIGB SHI'Z PFB BKF UHTTYIGEE, PFZ YZ SHI PFB BKF H BHSUZ PYW GIKFWU ZK TFXX FT DYWUZ HXKIWEYJG YZ.

—JHRYJ XGG DKZU

206. ICC VIKKXIZWE IKW LIFFS. XN'E NKSXBZ NQ CXDW NQZWNLWK IJNWKAIKGE NLIN MITEWE ICC NLW FKQOCWVE.

—ELWCCWS AXBNWKE

207. BR CBUC BUG KA LAAIG, WKUXRG KAT ZRQQUTG SK BSG LUESIJ OUG ZRQAC ZJ U LIUGB AL ISQBCKSKQ.

—CBAEUG LMIIRT

208. PZAAXFZZU CK V GAVTS FPSIS EPSX GAVTS XZJ JDUSI TZDEIVTE CDKESVU ZN JDUSI ZYKSIHVECZD.

—FVAESI FCDTPSAA

47

209. O QUFL IOXMBFLKLI WQUW UHH QSRUP

LFOH MBRLX AKBR WQOX: RUP'X NLOPY SPUNHL

WB XOW XWOHH OP U KBBR.   —NHUOXL ZUXMUH

210. DXTTGDP RG NB N'R KTXLA, HOP UZVL'P

PUG BNLG YNLG HGPKGGL VZLNPE ZLS RZSLGVV

AXPPGL BNLGT?   —AGXTAG WTNDG

211. YB QBI VBQYTEQ ILT ASYJETQI BU

NQBILTD CTVNSRT GI YGUUTDR UDBE HBSD BKQ.

HBS ENH CBIL CT KDBQJ.   —YNQYTEGR

212. CYGC ZK CXH YTC RW OYDZJS SAHKCK

WHHE YC XROH PXHJ CXYC'K THYEEV PXHTH VRA

PZKX CXHV PHTH.   —SHRTSH H. IHTSOYJ

213. ON XSAQA'M BTFVTA GOMXATOTD XV LSVY

O VLA YVTAF, O'Y CQACBQAZ XV NVQDAX OX ON

FVK BQA.   —AQQVG NGFTT

214. MYV DVMMVS XV KVVF WDRBM RBSTVFQVT,

MYV KVXVS MUEVT XV YWQV MR PHRZP TREVDRJL

VFTV JRXH MR KVVF MWFF.   —RJVMMW

48

215. CY AUP XZWRX WKWZA TCXPRXCUG RT R

SCYW-RGB-BWRXD ORXXWZ, AUP'SS BCW R SUX

UY XCOWT.   —BWRG TOCXD

216. WM DUOBP JRKBCWUO YROR GWDAPQ

MUPPUYWXN OSPRG, YR TUSPI AOUNOBD B

TUDASFRO FU JR DUOBP.   —GBDSRP A. NWXIRO

217. SXNWN ICGS ON GUINSXJAQ SU

ZHCVCAHSCWN—ZDSNW ZRR, EUC ANLNW GNN

ZAE GJHT VUWHCVJANG.   —OUO QUMMZWM

218. NABHGA PHCY JAHJEA CYUGY NHUCYXID

UNHRY YWAXG BUPXEZ YGAA, YWAZ RCRUEEZ MH

U DHHM JGRIXID VHN.   —H.U. NUYYXCYU

219. BZPZOW DYXX LHLT DYB SNL PUSSXL ZM

SNL ELVLE. SNLTL'E SZZ AIQN MTUSLTBYRYBJ

DYSN SNL LBLAW.   —NLBTW FYEEYBJLT

220. WJBC KENT IQJ CERTD IQJ'ON VSYFJYCNF

GSQH CEN BZEQQM QG NAUNSRNTZN, BQHNQTN

CERTDB JU Y TNK ZQJSBN.   —HYSI E. KYMFSRU

49

221. JITMPDTMJ N CMEJIF YNJ PI QI N KMEV

SIFQ GDJPNFHM IZP IB YDJ LNV PI HITM XNHO

N JYIEP GDJPNFHM HIEEMHPSV.

—MGLNEG NSXMM

222. N XOSL JNGECSLYLJ ZXL OYZ CU

JLELNSNBI JNMHCVOZG. N ZLHH ZXLV ZXL ZYWZX

OBJ ZXLF BLSLY TLHNLSL VL.

—EOVNHHC JN EOSCWY

223. NX XHHF SV RVYVGXVVG QVIWR XH PVX

XEWVV XEHJRIGK ENXR NG AIRVAIBB. N KNK NX

NG HGV IOXVWGHHG HG XEV PHBO ZHJWRV.

—EIGF IIWHG

224. GLV SKG QFDOE DQ'P K YLOU HKG JLHO

QFX TLKJ QL QFX JTVU PQLTX, MVQ QFKQ'P

WVPQ ZXKOVQP QL PZKRX.   —JLVUYKP KJKSP

225. ZCDZOC XBD TVFC BKRPDQL FIDX IDPBKIU

VMDNP BKRPDQL. LDN WVI RCC PBVP KI PBC

RDQP DS BKRPDQL PBCL TVFC.

—U.F. WBCRPCQPDI

226. KJUNIJ O ENS AGIIOJR, O CGR MOD

SCJNIOJM GKNWS KIOVEOVE WH FCOPRIJV; VNQ

O CGBJ MOD FCOPRIJV GVR VN SCJNIOJM.

—ZNCV QOPANS

227. M OML IUT SNQIW CUQ ITEPJ CUQ WMOQ

MC YNYCX MW UQ JNJ MC CIQLCX UMW IMWCQJ

CUNECX XQMEW TY UNW PNYQ. —OFUMOOMJ MPN

228. SV Y PORROJ-XJAOJOA UXJQA, RMO LZEGZ

TXRM UXFQA GMXU FE SV XIRXPOJ YVA OYR RMO

QOYKOG YNROJ RMOZ'KO NYQQOV.

—OAUYJA GROKOVGXV

229. GNS ZAAKDWZSKQQU DBVGRQN ZS BCN

BPVBC, RVB GZDB ZL BCNG EWAI BCNGDNQMND

VE KSX CVPPU ZLL KD WL SZBCWSJ CKX

CKEENSNX. —FWSDBZS ACVPACWQQ

230. DGXAWIHRMJGX, ONJDN JH HQBBGHWK MG

SW R MOG-ORT HMIWWM, JH MIWRMWK ST URXT

RH JY JM OWIW R KJAJKWK NJVNORT.

—UJHH URXXWIH

231. XRFVYKJL RZPJ LJPJK SJJL PJKW NMMY ZB VFABJLFLN BM BRJFK JVYJKA, SQB BRJW RZPJ LJPJK DZFVJY BM FUFBZBJ BRJU.

—CZUJA SZVYEFL

232. NJHEQ DK H ZJWB NSTT, NWJHWB HIIHDW, HGN RB HNZDLJ EU BUS DK EU QHZJ GUEQDGY PQHEJZJW EU NU PDEQ DE.

—P. KURJWKJE RHSYQHR

233. AC GXNJC IEXYCWQCY IL IEX USNWNRT RI VCR U GNFFU RI IEX JIIX OUYRCX RKUL UL UDSEWULHC.

—ANWW JEXYR

234. E GYRHZERHG VYPJHO ES ZNH RQPBSQIZBOHOG YS SYYAWOYYS EZHRG THHW Q SYYA YO ZVY YP ZNHEO WQFOYAA ZY ZHGZ ZNEPCG.

—QAQP IYOHP

235. AR UYGEFP QD RDI EL TPQ AUXXEPY: EM RDI MEHY U TDDY SEMP RDI'OO CP JUWWR; EM HDQ, RDI SEOO CPFDAP U WJEODLDWJPX.

—LDFXUQPL

236. KR UWFH JLHZV NZVZUVLWISH KU QWV

ZQQWGQNHX HPHLM FWLQKQJ, YH RHHT Z

NHLVZKQ PWKX. QWVSKQJ KQ VSH IZIHL VWXZM,

YH UKJS.   —TWLX ZNVWQ

237. QVZ FZIP TYP RDCVWCYO PV ALCY LD

RFKLJP. DV VDY RI RFKMYIIYO GRPA PAY

GVD-WVIP MYJVMO VU PAY MYUYMYY.

                    —XVAD A. AVWJVFH

238. QE QL G HOZGE SZTX YDO G AGW ED CZ QW

TDNZ MQES SQALZTY. YDO GW GREDO, SDMZNZO,

QE QL GCLDTJEZTI ZLLZWEQGT.

                    —ODCZOE ADOTZI

239. UOXZX JZX UOZXX EUJPXE CS KJW: OX

HXRTXAXE TW EJWUJ NRJME, OX QCXE WCU

HXRTXAX TW EJWUJ NRJME, OX TE EJWUJ

NRJME.   —HCH DOTRRTDE

240. IUH IARGYDH PFIU IHDDFWK Q KRRN JIRAV

FJ IUQI FI FWMQAFQYDV AHXFWNJ IUH RIUHA

EHDDRP RE Q NGDD RWH.   —JFN SQHJQA

241. BRAAVJB KJ VERK HQZTIE LR IVOR

HVAAVJB ZJ K MVJ. VA HQZTIE CKOR PZT WTCM

TM KJE EZ HZCRAQVJB. —R.I. HVCMHZJ

242. JM GME DMVVU TOMRE UMRV WVMONPIC

DZEA ITEAPITEZKC; Z TCCRVP UMR IZGP TVP BTV

SVPTEPV. —TNOPVE PZGCEPZG

243. WA WF HOART YIGC AH CWFAWTXZWFY

VRALRRT AYR BTHMBF HO EWOR ITC AYHFR HO

HNNHGAZTWAQ. —OGRCRGWMB NYWEEWNF

244. CGGCFVQWZVO ZI EZIINX HO ECIV GNCGUN

HNBDQIN ZV ZI XFNIINX ZW CYNFDUUI DWX

UCCRI UZRN LCFR. —VMCEDI NXZICW

245. ZWM YGXI ZWNGS ZWLZ VYGZNGKMA ZY

SNTM KA UYJM CYJ YKJ UYGMI NA ZWM

DMNSWNGS ULVWNGM. —SMYJSM VXLJO

246. OEIJ, WLDJRSZGDH, LJZHJTV SE REV

PRDVJ HJEHOJ NZ KPTG NZ N TEKKER GNVLJS

WEL ZEKJVGDRY. —NRVER TGJQGEI

54

247. KJW SEQRK XEXWVK HEQ CV CKJWMRK MR

SJWV JW HWWNR LQCKWHDN CVO JCR VE EVW KE

KJCVF. —SWVOG SCQO

248. LG SWMLOLZQ, LC EWH IDGO DGEONLGX

QDLF, DQV D KDG; LC EWH IDGO DGEONLGX

FWGJ, DQV D IWKDG. —KDPXDPJO ONDOZNJP

249. APM LBFEMEA AF QMGTMLAVFR I QMGEFR

MXMG LFHME VE NPMR PM TVBBE FZA I KFO

IQQBVLIAVFR TFGH. —EAIRBMC K. GIRSIBB

250. JD RIFVIE VIYR JO VI HVIC QMUAZN

AZVAJMVO RAZZOEH SIE SIWE. WZYOHH VQOEO

MEO VQEOO IVQOE COICYO. —IEHIZ LOYYOH

251. GH'T B ZSMSTTGPW ALSW IPCZ WSGDLEPZ

UPTST LGT KPE; GH'T B RSXZSTTGPW ALSW IPC

UPTS IPCZ PAW. —LBZZI T. HZCFBW

252. R NWJRS XRYK TJHTBJ SCZYD SCJK RWJ

SCZYDZYN QCJY SCJK RWJ XJWJBK WJRWWRYNZYN

SCJZW TWJAMOZPJL. —QZBBZRX ARXJL

55

253. B XALBE RV UROK B HKB SBM—JAF WBE'H HKUU PAX VHQAEM VPK RV FEHRU JAF IFH PKQ RE PAH XBHKQ. —EBEWJ QKBMBE

254. VUPQBTCZJN XZUBRI SR KP ZER HUJR, VTZ GPR ZEGTYEZ QRCZ SR JUOS; XGGP K'I VR ZGG CGGB ZG PRRI UP UPZK-ZERHZ UOUBS. —YKPU BGZEHROX

255. G YQUVRO AOQAYO XRQ HOOA TQDC. VROI ULO EQXULTC XRQ RUWOK'V DQV VRO DFVC VQ PGVO AOQAYO VROJCOYWOC. —UFDFCV CVLGKTPOLD

256. P MPYF RJIJWPZPBY WJDK JFHXGRPYU. JWJDK RPNJ ZBNJEBFK RHDYZ BY RSJ ZJR, P UB PYRB RSJ BRSJD DBBN GYF DJGF G EBBV. —UDBHXSB NGDO

257. UQHM KQAROMU ZCNQDKM SMKPAUM QG P HCUALZMDUVPLZCLT; QVIMDU, SMKPAUM VIMB ALZMDUVPLZ MPKI QVIMD VQQ JMOO. —MNPL MUPD

56

258. HPGBG VN WRAO WRG EVYYGBGRXG KGHJGGR Z QZEQZR ZRE QG. HPG QZEQZR HPVRCN PG VN NZRG. V CRWJ V ZQ QZE.

—NZASZEWB EZAV

259. SPUHXLMM OM SPUWOUKBDDN BQQPOUWOUH GBSW-GOUZOUH SPVVOWWLLM, CRLU CRBW CL XLBDDN ULLZ BXL MPVL GBSW-GBSOUH SPVVOWWLLM.

—XPHLX BDDLU

260. JQWAWPY WD AOU VPST RQVIUDDWVP JOUQU PV VPU HVPDWNUQD TVB QWNWHBSVBD WI TVB UEQP PV KVPUT.

—MBSUD QUPEQN

261. PWZXIO PI XIKYRLBIM RBRLBC QE KQIOCBWW MQ GQMB EQC MBCR JXRXMW XW JXZB PWZXIO P KTXKZBI MQ GQMB EQC KQJQIBJ WPIHBCW.

—LQL XIOJXW

262. OY TLX SNOZJ RLKH BQZ'S BLXZS, SPT VXSSOZK SNPUU RLK AOHBXOSH OZ TLXP VLBJUS QZR SNUZ KOCOZK YORL LZWT SML LY SNUG.

—VNOW VQHSLPUS

57

263. M GDZ'W HYJ DOBH GYH Y WDOCR HURDDN, KOW GX RYE DOB DGZ UDBDZXB. GX OHXE WD GBMWX XHHYJH NMVX "GRYW M'S CDMZC WD KX MI M CBDG OF."   —NXZZJ KBOUX

264. ZOVMFAJK WVOFAER VMLU MJZ VYVOS GJV GQ XR EG IV NXAVEBS MJZ RMQVBS AJRMJV VYVOS JAKUE GQ GXO BAYVR.

—DABBAMF ZVFVJE

265. GO GJ ECDZO OH MD Z MQHTAD. VGOP QHV DSXDLOZOGHTJ GO'J RDCU DZJU OH JWCXCGJD XDHXQD.   —XZKDQZ ZTADCJHT

266. NCD NBK QDOYWPH TDAWGDF UKT FRAADFF OTD XRWQYWPH O XDNNDT LKRFDNTOG OPY UWPYWPH O XWHHDT QKKGCKQD.

—DYHOT O. FACKOUU

267. QBCCYM JPM BA GJNBWP J HGKBHM RMIXMMW IXK IMQOIJIBKWA JWC HGKKABWP IGM KWM IGJI'YY PMI EKV GKQM MJLYBML.

—CJW RMWWMII

58

268. OV NCGNAC ZCKAAS AODCE PG XGZD, XC'E IPOAA RC NAGXOBL PQC AKBE XOPQ IPOUDI KBE PZKBINGZPOBL LGGEI GB GHZ RKUDI.

—XOAAOKY VCKPQCZ

269. TSEPX MNDXOB PAN YTN KXHW LANPYSANB KX NPAYT YTPY PHHKZ YTNDA LTDHJANX YK LKEN MPLI TKEN.

—MDHH LKBMW

270. Y ZXV'W NOAD QEOW GXT UOG OIXTW SD, OU RXVC OU GXT UOG UXSDWEYVC OIXTW SD, OVZ OU RXVC OU GXT UFDRR SG VOSD AYCEW.

—CDXACD S. NXEOV

271. GAQ CLKQ GY DJRNGA IGCQ NIMGCRDAR RODA DKK GROQCE JGAENERE NA AQSQC BGNAU DAHRONAU RODR EGIQGAQ QKEQ JDA BG YGC HGL.

—JDKSNA JGGKNBUQ

272. R LJS'D YRQQ IQRKB TGD R QRYK DJ XKBB FRDZ DZKRV XRSLB. R ZJQL DZKX ETJPK NQJTKB. DZKO IVKEY JGD ESL OKQQ, "FZJE, R'X FEO DJJ ZRNZ!"

—TVGHK TEGX

59

273. PJR XRYBPE AL JYKWIC Y OAU WIHAFR WT PJYP PJRGR WT IAP RIABCJ FAIRE PA XBE UJYP EAB QAI'P GRYOOE IRRQ. —GYE WIFYI

274. NKLGT HKFRGSN JB GCKFOKFI JB VFT OKFY KN ZJRFY GJ MSVY GJ AJFBRNKJF VFY RFCVWWKFSNN. —XVHSN GCREZSE

275. PNZGZ'E DVPNODS JGVDS JOPN EVMPNZGD XTKOBVGDOT PNTP T GOEZ OD PNZ VXZTD KZYZK JVMKCD'P XMGZ. —GVEE RTXCVDTKC

276. K'N DAZEUILWG BZJVT JR AXL YZKUFWLD K XEQL. YXEA K'N IKQKUI VB KU LWEDAKOKAG, K'N IEKUKUI KU YKDTJN. —DVCEUUL DJNLZD

277. QMVY BRIBGR LI ORMCTL FGIXRL LIIHX CX FRHYVCTGK TIY JK FITFRHT DTGRXX C'J ORMCTL YMRHR QCYM 'RJ. —LIGGK BVHYIT

278. RXIIJXHD JE ZJND X UJCZJT. XQBDI BLD SDXWBJQWZ RWEJV JE CUDI, BLD EBIJTHE XID EBJZZ XBBXVLDA. —FXVCS SIXWAD

279. EK JXXMKO GU WI EK EGO LKKS ZXAFKO

WSNX EWU DJXNEKU GSO EGO IXFQXNNKS NX

UGR "PEKS." —Z.Q. PXOKEXAUK

280. X'DN HNDNA SNNH FNQKITV. HIY NDNH

OUNH BL PQP MXHXVUNP YUN MXMYU CAQPN Q

LNQA SNMIAN X PXP. —FNMM MIJOIAYUL

281. WIY ABYNZXWI: XD ZQXN XN ZQY

XIDWLVEZXWI ETY, QWK GWVY IWHWMO PIWKN

EIOZQXIT? —LWHYLZ VEIPWDD

282. AJD SVRJA AF UD JDMSC CFDO YFA

MXAFNMAVBMQQK VYBQXCD AJD SVRJA AF UD

AMLDY ODSVFXOQK. —JXUDSA J. JXNGJSDK

283. RSJQQ W'UNWUD HM CNXCKM RWW NCRQ WJ

RWW QCJNK VWJ CBKRSHBF KWG XCBR RW IW.

—ZQCB-YCGN MCJRJQ

284. MEBJJBC DJ XLB USH NLP, LSQDHA

HPXLDHA XP JSV, SMJXSDHJ KFPU ADQDHA

NPFCV BQDCBHYB PK XLB KSYX. —ABPFAB BEDPX

285. BDM JMHYJGYSKM BDTIQ YSUCB

ODYGMOEMYJM TO BDYB DM JMYKKF TO RMJF

QUUZ, TI OETBM UN YKK BDM EMUEKM LDU OYF

DM TO RMJF QUUZ. —JUSMJB QJYRMO

286. UJ AMPL TQD Q DKMNTE MUYLGMULVE MV

TLI DYLLRT. LFLIJ VSA QVG ETLV DTL DESYD ES

ZILQETL. —BMUUJ GXIQVEL

287. GYNLN'H KODM KON UZM GK YZPN Z YZTTM

IZLLVZEN ZOW ZH HKKO ZH V DNZLO UYZG VG

VH V'DD ENG IZLLVNW ZEZVO.

—QDVOG NZHGUKKW

288. UP ADUBPDB, LVB DQBZUL WJBA LJ LVB

EKP OVJ DJPTUPDBA LVB OJQMZ, PJL LJ OVJE

LVB UZBK XUQAL JDDSQA.

—AUQ XQKPDUA ZKQOUP

289. FKLTL LQBZFZ XU YUWBFBRBMX BX BXVBM

VMTBXI LXUJIK FU MFFLGYF FU LQYWMBX FU FKL

GMZZLZ FKMF RUHZ RMX CL LMFLX.

—BXVBTM IMXVKB

62

290. X HDFCVQLTFZ NCWACCV DCZRDWCD XVQ LRIDSC KXLWL RVKP IVWFK FW FL ZDRHFWXNKC HRD RVC WR NCWDXP WTC RWTCD.

—UXIDCCV QRAQ

291. IUMDADXDJQR JVC ICUIMC ZNU, ZNCQ ANCE RCC MDLNA JA ANC CQG US ANC AHQQCM, LU UHA JQG KHE RUFC FUVC AHQQCM.

—PUNQ THDQAUQ

292. XDCWPWTWUJG UIH PVH GUAH UCC DLHI. PVHO XIDAWGH PD SQWCB U SIWBEH HLHJ MVHIH PVHIH WG JD IWLHI.

—JWFWPU FVIQGVTVHL

293. LW LY OSW ESPWC IO LOWGDDLXGOW HIO'Y WLHG WS FG LO WCG HIRSPLWT. FT JGULOLWLSO, WCGPG IPG IDPGIJT GOSNXC QGSQDG WS JS WCIW.

—X.C. CIPJT

294. EFQLGRP GQ LZP GIQFSDIRP YP ZDXP UI UFS CGXPQ, DIB UMPBGPIRP GQ LZP WSPNGFN YP WDH VUS GL.

—YGCCGDN WPII

63

295. BR BD I JIEUGSMOD RLBEU QMS I
EIRBMEIV PIEJBJIRG RM DIX RLBEUD RLIR
FGMFVG YBULR SGYGYCGS. —GOUGEG YPPISRLX

296. SP AXM NSC PSKL CA SXACZMY: FKYCZLSUP
SYM HKQM EVY FSHHP—CZM JAYM UAV ZSGM,
CZM JAYM UAV OSO. —JSYHS JAYOSX

297. EGGO JGVVZRNJDHNGR NI DI IHNVZSDHNRE
DI LSDJB JGAAQQ, DRO MZIH DI WDXO HG ISQQY
DAHQX. —DRRQ VGXXGP SNROLQXEW

298. Z OSWZSPS IYRVWM ISVQVR XVR TVES GNZC
XYARGIK UNVG ZG YRXS UVC ... V WVIQS VIXGZX
ISQZYR XYPSISM UZGN ZXS. —CGSPS TVIGZR

299. VZS KESGV VZDFK GHUBV NSWUOEGOQ DX
VZGV DV KDMSX SMSEQ MUVSE G OZGFOS VU NU
XUWSVZDFK XVBJDN. —GEV XJGFNSE

300. VUGYV ELTUCVL ZGQP DGEL M FUYRFGPYFP
GR ZGNP ATGXGYV OUCT FMT DGEL ELP KTMNPR
UY. —KCAA RFLCZKPTV

64

301. TQCDEJDKYTGPW JU TA QAYJZTHNR
ZNPJIHN XDY CNHHJAK CPN CYQCP TEDQC DCPNY
GNDGHN. —GPJHJG KQNRTHHT

302. ZYL PRYX ZYL QMJ DMYXGRD YWE XTJR
QWFYVB JAJMZBTGRD TLMBV, QRE XTQB EYJV
RYB TLMB EYJV RYB XYMP. —TZ DQMERJM

303. XBUV ZLRS KSTBE TJ IRFO TYYVEYBLE TJ
ZLR CL ZLRS OTBS, TEC ZLR'QQ KV T YOLRJTEC
YBIVJ KVYYVS LMM. —ITQFLQI A

304. YA RYZZYGU CEO DVM EGOCMB, CM'K VEWM
OPZWMK EZZ PIB XBPLZMHO E ZPGU DYHM EUP.

—KYTR UBMUPBJ

305. GMXZSBT ZG KZVS E GBSR. ZQ TMA NMF'B
VSSU ZB GBZOOSN AU, TMA LSB E KMB MQ GXAY
MF BMU. —SNREON EHHST

306. XGTBZVVZ ETCKCXZ, AGTUQVI PALXKVLPZH,
NZLXK: C ELX'P YZVCZBZ C SLCH XCXZPI-KCR
HGVVLAK LXH C'N KPCVV QTXUAI. —NCMZ MLVCX

307. PFKOK EOK UXQL PSU TQEGGKG UB MKZKGPOWEXG WX PFKGK ZELG UB OKTDQKGG IUPUO POEBBWT—PFK CHWTD EXZ PFK ZKEZ.

—PFUIEG OUJKOP ZKSEO

308. AT AZC JBBZVQJFZU YUZVATV JY VQUTFBT KAZK HZCT AQV BJFMTGVZKQJF OTGYTBKUW CTUQIAKYXU.

—VWCFTW VHQKA

309. W HDR'S NTJDZ QKO DRP KSUJO XDOOWDYJ, MFS SUJ NJHOJS KQ KFO XDOOWDYJ WN SUDS VJ UDAJ DMNKCFSJCP RKSUWRY WR HKXXKR.

—XDXWJ JWNJRUKVJO

310. HGV HY LUV OVBBHGB HY USBLHKA SB LUDL GHLUSGW SB HYLVG D WHHT LUSGW LH TH DGT DOQDAB D JOVIVK LUSGW LH BDA.

—QSOO TCKDGL

311. O HOR KXXCMGDU YGWE MCVTGX KS KWEDS GHMKSWORW VCJGRDJJ XORRKW, ORU RDDU RKW, OWWDRU WK JMDTTGRQ.

—ROMKTDKR VKROMOSWD

66

312. RW ASJXPEJVIDS'T J HBVVHD ECSADVEGH,

OGV ID HBQDT VC ABND RD JPNBYD. CXD PJW,

ID VCCQ RD JTBPD JXP HDEV RD VIDSD.

—SCX SBYIJSPT

313. HXQ SMESKIQ KZ G UJFQEGU QLMDGHJKB

JI HK VGRQ PKM SXJUKIKSXJDGU QBKMYX HK

GDDQSH HXQ ZGDH HXGH PKM TJUU BQAQE VGRQ

VMDX VKBQP.
—BKEVGB LKMYUGI

314. DI DP'V E GDTT, PRS KYVP YIIDOS MDTT

HSP DP PY LYJ DF PMSFPL-IYJW RYJWV. DI DP'V

E ORSOU, ETTYM PRSA E OYJKTS MSSUV.

—WDOREWQ FSSQREA

315. Z XSZSDXSDVDZC DX XFGQFCQ YIF DX NFFU

ZS KDNJPQX WJS YIF UFQXC'S IZAQ SIQ

BQPXFCZEDST SF WQ ZC ZVVFJCSZCS.

—PFT ITUQ

316. EBWD QC R SPRXD GBA ZMBJ AS JRKNQKZ

NB PDRLD, RKU ZMBJ BPU JRKNQKZ NB ZDN

HRXV NB.
—YBEK DU SQDMXD

67

317. KW NICJI BN DUPJ UW UEEHJ EKJ RIND
MGIUBGS, ONL DLMB RKIMB GIJUBJ BSJ
LWKAJIMJ. —GUIH MUQUW

318. WUD KOZPWK OJLD PDTZPCK ODZOSD'K
JTTZGOSFKUGDVWK, WUD NPZVW OJLD VZWUFVL
MIW WUDFP NJFSIPDK. —EIKWFTD DJPS RJPPDV

319. ZHDW LHFTBWZ RH HCWA QKWPA XFORWQZ
CWAS LEAWYFBBS WCWAS DHIQK; HQKWAZ NFZQ
RH HCWA QKWD. —ZEBBS THTBPI

320. TVMQDI UESKR QU CHZKEJM ELC UZOC
ELQDI ZU ISQDI ES Z KZUQDS, SDJM PQEL DS
KSKREZQJ UCGAQKC. —ECB ZJJCD

321. RPA QOZX BAVHQO TPQ ZKHRAOH RQ MQRP
HKJAH QD YO YVFSGAOR KH RPA DAZZQT KO RPA
OAUR YBYVRGAOR. —VSRP MVQTO

322. KLJVGKZ GH HL MDPCWWCHHGKZ CH
TCJSVGKZ HLDMLKM YL HLDMJVGKZ JVCJ RLQ
HCGY SLQUYK'J PM YLKM. —HCD MTGKZ

68

323. TG TV OHEHD'V GPE HXHNVETNTVF OH'Z

RXX AH ORVNJTDQ VHXHCTUTPD AF

NRDZXHXTQJV. —QHPEQH QPAHX

324. LS HDKBSQ HRGBYXS HVKBGDXQK DXVYFQ

TVNQJRKL MVENK BV PDZS BLS TVNQJRKL BLRFZ

BLSA ESXS TVRFT HNDGSK. —JXSQ DNNSF

325. Z CVZMM CWJ W ENAPEN CVDDIMD OZVN W

MZKNVYZYK PLT LY VLI CNLOC W MWES LB

ELYBZTDYED. —TLAK HWEMDLT

326. DZMLN ML IXZ TOPR MW EMAZ DZMLN ML

IXZ DGR WFGHIW, ZKFZYI IXTI IXZ DGR WFGHIW

XTJZ TCHEI WHYZOJMWMGL. —DETAZ FETOA

327. F QXMAG TH DJTRTKVJQ MQMFEEG

BDPDFEQ XIFX XID SDQX XVKD XT SMG FRGXIVRZ

VQ EFQX GDFB. —KFBXG FEEDR

328. T DBZNV ACUCL LCPV P GBBF TO TW DCLC

IBJJTGNC OBL RC WB WPNF EPNO PA EBZL DTWE

WEC RPA DEB DLBWC TW. —DBBVLBD DTNJBA

329. LC'Q SMTH JGT CSW RGHWTZ VWZWTMCLGZ

CG IZHWTQCMZH CSGTWMI, XSG ELAWH DWQLHW

M KGZH DIC HLHZ'C GXZ XMCWT QOLQ GT M

QZGTOWE.   —DLEE AMIVSMZ

330. CKEHQNF QN R ZAKKI HRKEAREC. JFRJ

CDMHRQKN UFI UC MROW GAO XRO GK JFC

LOQYCURI RKL LOQYC GAO XRO GK JFC

MROWURI.   —TROW EORNNG

331. AQXGRO OEZXR IR. G UJL'F VZLF FJ SQF

IT PZGFD GL SRJSWR VDJ VRXRL'F OIZXF

RLJQBD FJ BRF JQF JP AQXT UQFT.

                                      —IJLGEZ SGSRX

332. WKRVR FZ SN UNFSW HW MKFEK ONY EHS

ZHO, "MRQQ, F'G ZYEERZZLYQ SNM. F GFAKW HZ

MRQQ WHJR H SHU."   —EHVVFR LFZKRV

333. CJU SUIODB CJUSU ISU OD QUN QUPIMU

RDMGCGHGIBO GO CJIC GC GO CDD PVHJ

CSDVLMU CD RVC PIXU-VR DB CND QIHUO.

                                      —PIVSUUB PVSRJT

334. S XSBPQPXB PX S VSL GJU RPXTUYNQX

HLEWNSXSLB BJPLCX SFUHB JPVXNWK SLR BJNL

XSDX BJNV SFUHB UBJNQ ENUEWN.

—ENBNQ VTSQBJHQ

335. EGEDWU-EGED XDZFDEW HA WLD XDHXYD

GE WLD JHZYO RZD AHHYK, REO WLD ZDKW HA

SK RZD GE NZDRW ORENDZ HA FHEWRNGHE.

—WLHZEWHE JGYODZ

336. YGN CITSHYWBAN SU W TZDPCA MTNWRNH

DNWHM WB CBJNHMN HNPWYCSBMGCT YS YGN

BZIDNH SU ICAHSTGSBNM CBYS VGCAG GN

MTNWRM. —VCPPCWI ISHXWB

337. NG'A FYG GKUG N BMNGI BIEE, N DXAG

LYF'G BMNGI QULEW RIMW YZGIF, UFL GKUG

OUAAIA ZYM HYYL YF GIEIRNANYF.

—UFLW MYYFIW

338. JEB R.I. AI JEB DPUM WDRPJNM KEBNB

TXAURNB JD ZNDCDJB MDRNIBUT AI KALBUM

WDPIALBNBL XNNDOXPJ. —OXNNM JNRLBXR

339. VI MVI ZM ZDI PJQQNI KEIU ZDI VMXUZ ZVM JYLIYZJMYU MS DRPKYJZT—XMPKYZJW NMLI KYQ ERY CMVQIX.   —KYQXI PKRXMJU

340. G'W ICKRVLSXVZ KLUX SPXUX GK AR VGDX RA WIUK. GS'K ARS VGKSXQ RA WZ QILFPSXU'K BPRAX CGVV.   —VIUUZ WISSPXJK

341. ICK YBYCA, PCOY DA MIJ POOLVVYR, OIC NY XIRY AP IEEYIV DCYBDAINSY NK I OPXEYAYCA MDJAPVDIC.   —SYY JDXPCJPC

342. UQ MHNIO EHMA XHFYNJAX UA YT OGA WNYCTXI YM HTJYUSVOHRHDHOQ, VTX RAIHXAI H OGHTZ IGA GVOAX UA.   —YIJVN DAFVTO

343. X SNISWPKU NO FSA BNEV KL QAPOKE USK GKKBO XF X OXROXIA XEV FSNEBO KL QNMXOOK.   —XGXE QXFPNMB SAPWAPF

344. NTGA XI PD QLZAXWIA GPVXAXLC? X'OW GQNGDI NGCAWE AL ATYLN GC WJJ XCAL GC WQWMAYXM ZGC.   —LQXOWY TWYZLYE

345. UX AVK CMCO GCC HC WCPPULW RCFPCL RA PYC BVTUSC, BKP IVZL PYC MUICV SFHCOF FLI SVHC YCTB HC. —RVRSFP WVTIPYZFUP

346. LO'G FZMAOJ LSG PSEO WMIZAJ. LO ZGOJ FI DO KSGOMWDPO WAJ JOCMOGGOJ, AIR LO'G JOCMOGGOJ WAJ KSGOMWDPO. —JWBSJ EMIGF

347. WBQAQ KAQ FDYQ SGQKF FD HADVN WBKW DVCL K MQAL SVWQCCSNQVW IQAFDV EDJCG ZQCSQMQ WBQY. —NQDANQ DAHQCC

348. GQJO OS PQKY RSFY AVJ? RYJB RSFYSJY Q OYDYXNQF RQCZJX, "ZXJSNY AZNRO OYDYXNQF." —PYJJC CSVJXFQJ

349. ECMVPEUV EPV: E TPLFRUV LQ VAS RWVEKSWVSF MLKF CG VAS RWTPOWUOTKSF VL VAS RVVSPKG CSZOKFSPSF. —EK UETT

350. Y'J ZQHRB HA ZMUYEI FMNGV. FSG HECU FSYEI YV—Y WHRCB XG KRVF MV ZQHRB AHQ SMCA FSG JHEGU. —MQFSRQ IHBAQGU

73

351. JBF ITYO R JTERP JTUM HYP FYRUO HT

ABRPXY R ERP'O BRCVHO RPI HBYP ATELWRVP

HBRH BY'O PTH HBY ERP OBY ERUUVYI?

—CRUCUR OHUYVORPI

352. BXMDXKORB U SRM R OPW. DPORB U'Y R

OPW. DPYPKKPS U'ZZ NKPEREZB MDUZZ EX R

OPW. MUWC! DCXKX'M MP ZUDDZX CPNX JPK

ROHRFIXYXFD. —MFPPNB

353. SCZUDPZZ UZ DPMPO ZX LPRFJLI RZ BLPD,

FUVP R GLUGVPD, UJ TCZJ QX R GPOJRUD

RTXCDJ XK ZGORJGLUDH KXO BLRJ UJ HPJZ.

—LPDOI KXOQ

354. FZT GLQQTNTZXT VTSATTZ GTPSU PZG

SPRTD LD SUPS GTPSU GFTDZ'S HTS AFNDT

TYTNE SLIT XFZHNTDD ITTSD. —NFE DXUPTQTN

355. LU K RWS QLUEZWP K GTQXEZWY GKU

QKCW K QLPZKCW PT NYWKZ ZOKZ LZ STEDM

ZKCW QKUV QWU QKUV QTUZOP ZT WBEKD LZ.

—QWYDW. D. QWKGOKQ

74

356. F JGPKE XDWZMX WZDW WZM VMGVKM

JGHEMX JZA F JDCH'W VXMCFEMHW WZDH JZA F

DS. —CDKSGH V. UZDCM

357. EGNC R VRC FNDUFNZ RCL DUVN UZ CQ

WQCXNF QS TFXNCD UVIQFDRCHN, GUZ

HQWWNRXTNZ XNCNFRWWJ IFNZNCD GUV EUDG R

ERDHG. —F.H. ZGNFFUSS

358. SAPF P XVFZ ABHPG YMVGRQ EPG'F

MKEAPGRM XTDYWMHQ. MCMTZDGM LGDSQ

MKPEFWZ ADS FD QDWCM FAM DFAMT

OMWWDS'Q. —DWVG HVWWMT

359. VL USK TSH'M PVHT WPYNNVHD NVAY

IYZHKM OKMMYQ LSQ MRS SQ MEQYY TZUW,

IYZHKM OKMMYQ VW TZQH DSST WEZXVHD

FQYZP. —OZQQU DSNTRZMYQ

360. SERI VZTNL IEOGW IERI IEK SEKKV SRM

OGXKGIKB HKPJYK IEK RZIJCJHOVK; JIEKYSOMK,

TRG LJZ OCRWOGK IEK RSPZV MTYKKTEOGW?

—MRCZKV EJPPKGMIKOG

75

361. T'P F WUNPULSVJ. LSFL'Z F WJVFL LSTQW

LU EV, F WUNPULSVJ. ZSV BFAAZ PV WUN MUJ

ZSUJL. LSFL'Z BYLV. T LFYWSL SVJ LSFL.

—VAAVQ NVWVQVJVZ

362. MHW YIHZ ZUJI MHW'FJ MHWIN, MHW

LUVIY MHWF ARA'T TWGJFERI. LUJI MHW NFHZ

WG RIA FJRKVPJ UJ'T DWTL R FJNWKRF NWM

ZUH ZJRFT R BRGJ. —ARSJ RLJKK

363. TZ TM UKII ZP FKRKRLKF ZOJZ ZOK

KWZTFK XWTYKFMK, UTZO PWK ZFTBITWH

KAEKNZTPW, TM EPRNPMKC PB PZOKFM.

—DPOW JWCFKU OPIRKM

364. SF'L OPLF BL LPGI B GINSJI QDG QBSVPGI

FD ABTI FAI GSZAF SEIB QSQFW WIBGL FDD

LDDX BL QSTI WIBGL FDD VBFI. —O.G. JVBFF

365. EGGZSIMM VBPGARGAIZNO ZQN ZXG XGAOZ

NMNWNBZO GE IWNAVPIB OGPVNZJ: YVGMNBPN

RTBPZTIZNH SJ PGWWVZZNN WNNZVBCO.

—CNGACN XVMM

76

366. A Q T D R S P J M   P C   R   E J M Q A X B T Z   S O P M I .   P B

H J T   D J T Z Q M ' S   C P I M   H J T X   M R G A   H J T ' Q   O R W A   S J

U R H   D R C O .   —X P S R   G R A   K X J E M

367. V K R Y X   S V   V Y L N H   W K E N   D E Y S I H   V K   C S T T

K Z V   V J N   S I O K W N   V Y M   C K E W   V J Y I   S V   R K N H   V K

W Y L N   V J N   S I O K W N .   —Y T C E N R   N .   I N Z W Y I

368. E S R T W T G S ,   P Q S   F G D O   N V F J S Z Z T F G   P Q M P

D M A F V Z   T G W S Z Z M G P D O   P F   R S Z P V F O   P Q S   V S M Z F G

J F V   T P Z   S H T Z P S G W S .   —I M E S Z   A V O W S

369. T L H T K L   D K U D Q V   M H E L   B T   W H   E L   D Z J   V D Q

W A D W   E Q   V E H F N Z O   N V   C H W A L X N Z O   W A L E .   U L K K

N W ' V   F N K K N Z O   E L !   —U L Z J Q   K N L C E D Z

370. K   Q R D   D G F   C K V V   W R E   Z A   I N E Q F E A .   P R J   K

O P R J   J G H D   D G R I F   M R T D R E I   J F E F   J F H E K P Q   Z H I O I

W R E .   —U H Z F I   G .   C R E F P

1. I have the perfect simplified tax form for the government. Why don't they just print our money with a return address on it? —*Bob Hope*

2. The scientific theory I like best is that the rings of Saturn are composed entirely of lost airline luggage. —*Mark Russell*

3. The trouble with jogging is that, by the time you realize you're not in shape for it, it's too far to walk back. —*Franklin P. Jones*

4. Patience is something you admire in the driver behind you, and scorn in the one ahead. —*Mac McCleary*

5. Your assumptions are your windows on the world. Scrub them off every once in a while, or the light won't come in. —*Alan Alda*

6. Know yourself. Don't accept your dog's admiration as conclusive evidence that you are wonderful. —*Ann Landers*

7. They say such nice things about people at their funerals that it makes me sad that I'm going to miss mine by just a few days. —*Garrison Keillor*

8. It's amazing that the amount of news that happens in the world every day always just exactly fits the newspaper. —*Jerry Seinfeld*

9. Don't knock the weather; nine-tenths of the people couldn't start a conversation if it didn't change once in a while. —*Kin Hubbard*

10. Anytime four New Yorkers get into a cab together without arguing, a bank robbery has just taken place. —*Johnny Carson*

11. An economist is an expert who will know tomorrow why the things he predicted yesterday didn't happen. —*Earl Wilson*

12. After being on the road so much I want to spend more time with my family, who I hear are wonderful people. —*Howie Mandel*

13. How can you be expected to govern a country that has two hundred and forty-six kinds of cheese? —*Charles de Gaulle*

14. Life is like a B-movie. You don't want to leave in the middle of it, but you don't want to see it again. —*Ted Turner*

15. We were so poor we had no hot water. But it didn't matter because we had no bathtub to put it in anyway. —*Tom Dreesen*

16. The average pencil is seven inches long, with just a half-inch eraser—in case you thought optimism was dead. —*Robert Brault*

17. Bill Clinton's foreign policy experience stems mainly from having breakfast at the International House of Pancakes. —*Pat Buchanan*

18. There should be some schools called deformatories to which people are sent if they are too good to be practical. —*Samuel Butler*

19. My job is to talk to you, and your job is to listen. If you finish first, please let me know. —*Harry Hershfield*

20. One of my chief regrets during my years in the theater is that I couldn't sit in the audience and watch me. —*John Barrymore*

21. I went to a restaurant that serves breakfast at any time. So I ordered French toast during the Renaissance. —*Steven Wright*

22. This will never be a civilized country until we spend more money for books than we do for chewing gum. —*Elbert Hubbard*

23. Thanks to the Interstate Highway System, it is now possible to travel from coast to coast without seeing anything. —*Charles Kuralt*

24. Did you ever walk in a room and forget why you walked in? I think that's how dogs spend their lives. —*Sue Murphy*

25. Ideas are like rabbits. You get a couple and learn how to handle them, and pretty soon you have a dozen. —*John Steinbeck*

26. I haven't reported my missing credit card to the police because whoever stole it is spending less than my wife. —*Ilie Nastase*

27. You can easily judge the character of a man by how he treats those who can do nothing for him. —*James D. Miles*

28. The best way to keep children home is to make the home atmosphere pleasant—and let the air out of the tires. —*Dorothy Parker*

29. Why should people go out and pay to see bad movies when they can stay at home and see bad television for nothing? —*Samuel Goldwyn*

30. Asking a working writer what he thinks about critics is like asking a lamppost how it feels about dogs. —*Christopher Hampton*

31. I'd like to see the government get out of war altogether and leave the whole field to private industry. —*Joseph Heller*

32. Disney, of course, has the best casting. If he doesn't like an actor he simply tears him up. —*Alfred Hitchcock*

33. I asked each senator about his preferences for the presidency, and ninety-six senators each received one vote. —*John F. Kennedy*

34. Middle age: when you're home on Saturday night, the telephone rings, and you hope it's the wrong number. —*Ring Lardner*

35. I think men who have a pierced ear are better prepared for marriage. They've experienced pain and bought jewelry. —*Rita Rudner*

36. You're only here for a short visit. Don't hurry. Don't worry. And be sure to smell the flowers along the way. —*Walter Hagen*

37. Millions long for immortality who do not know what to do with themselves on a rainy Sunday afternoon. —*Susan Ertz*

38. If you owe your bank a hundred pounds, you have a problem; but if you owe your bank a million, it has. —*John Maynard Keynes*

39. The fastest way to succeed is to look as if you are playing by other people's rules, while quietly playing by your own. —*Michael Korda*

40. Lots of people think they're charitable if they give away their old clothes and things they don't want. *—Myrtle Reed*

41. There's so much plastic in this culture that vinyl leopard skin is becoming an endangered synthetic. *—Lily Tomlin*

42. If you live to the age of a hundred you have it made because very few people die past the age of a hundred. *—George Burns*

43. Harpists spend about ninety percent of their lives tuning their harps and ten percent playing out of tune. *—Igor Stravinsky*

44. Instead of giving a politician the keys to the city, it might be better to change the locks. *—Doug Larson*

45. Hollywood's a place where they'll pay you a thousand dollars for a kiss, and fifty cents for your soul. *—Marilyn Monroe*

46. Of the seven dwarfs, only Dopey had a shaven face. This should tell us something about the custom of shaving. *—Tom Robbins*

47. I have left orders to be awakened at any time in case of national emergency, even if I'm in a cabinet meeting. *—Ronald Reagan*

48. A straight line may be the shortest distance between two points, but it is by no means the most interesting. *—Doctor Who*

49. I'm paranoid about everything. On my stationary bicycle I have a rearview mirror. *—Richard Lewis*

50. A good listener is not someone with nothing to say. A good listener is a good talker with a sore throat. *—Katharine Whitehorn*

51. Finishing second in the Olympics gets you silver. Finishing second in politics gets you oblivion. *—Richard Milhous Nixon*

52. I am not willing to risk the lives of German soldiers for countries whose names we cannot spell properly. *—Volker Ruhe*

53. The longest word in the English language is the one that follows the phrase, "And now a word from our sponsor." *—Hal Eaton*

54. Even more exasperating than the guy who thinks he knows it all is the one who really does. *—Al Bernstein*

55. I once bought my kids a set of batteries for Christmas with a note on it saying, "Toys not included." *—Bernard Manning*

56. Children are the most desirable opponents at Scrabble as they are both easy to beat and fun to cheat. *—Fran Lebowitz*

57. New York City now leads the world's greatest cities in the number of people around whom you shouldn't make a sudden move.

—David Letterman

58. Why do birds sing in the morning? It's the triumphant shout: "We got through another night." *—Enid Bagnold*

59. We who officially value freedom of speech above life itself seem to have nothing to talk about but the weather. —*Barbara Ehrenreich*

60. Ask a man which way he is going to vote, and he will probably tell you. Ask him, however, why, and vagueness is all. —*Bernard Levin*

61. Cleaning your house while your kids are still growing is like shoveling the walk before it stops snowing. —*Phyllis Diller*

62. A compromise is the art of dividing a cake in such a way that everyone believes he has the biggest piece. —*Ludwig Erhard*

63. I'm a philosophy major. That means I can think deep thoughts about being unemployed. —*Bruce Lee*

64. In Hollywood, an equitable divorce settlement means each party getting fifty percent of the publicity. —*Lauren Bacall*

65. Hard work and a proper frame of mind prepare you for the lucky breaks that finally come along—or don't. —*Harrison Ford*

66. I've gained a few pounds around the middle. The only lower-body garments I own that still fit me comfortably are towels. —*Dave Barry*

67. Never brag about your ancestors coming over on the Mayflower; the immigration laws weren't as strict in those days. —*Lew Lehr*

68. It's strange how few of the world's great problems are solved by people who remember their algebra. —*Herbert Prochnow*

69. True love comes quietly, without banners or flashing lights. If you hear bells, get your ears checked. —*Erich Segal*

70. If you don't want to work, you have to work to earn enough money so that you won't have to work. —*Ogden Nash*

71. Imagination is a good horse to carry you over the ground—not a flying carpet to set you free from probability. —*Robertson Davies*

72. Adults are always asking little kids what they want to be when they grow up—'cause they're looking for ideas. —*Paula Poundstone*

73. A tourist is a fellow who drives thousands of miles so he can be photographed standing in front of his car. —*Emile Ganest*

74. Isn't it strange? The same people who laugh at gypsy fortune tellers take economists seriously. —*Cincinnati Enquirer*

75. Anyone who says businessmen deal in facts, not fiction, has never read old five-year projections. —*Malcolm Forbes*

76. I'm tired of all this nonsense about beauty being only skin deep. That's deep enough. What do you want, an adorable pancreas? —*Jean Kerr*

77. History teaches us that men and nations behave wisely once they have exhausted all other alternatives. —*Abba Eban*

78. They are doing away with drive-ins. Now where are the teenagers going to go to not watch a movie? —*Bob Thomas*

81

79. Only one person in a thousand is a bore, and he is interesting because he is one person in a thousand. —*Harold Nicolson*

80. Half of our life is spent trying to find something to do with the time we have rushed through life trying to save. —*Will Rogers*

81. The advantage of having a bad memory is that, several times over, one enjoys the same good things for the first time.—*Friedrich Nietzsche*

82. Okay, so God made man first, but doesn't everyone make a rough draft before they make a masterpiece? —*Courtney Huston*

83. My initial response was to sue her for defamation of character, but then I realized that I had no character. —*Charles Barkley*

84. Midlife crisis is that moment when you realize your children and your clothes are about the same age. —*Bill Tammeus*

85. Computers will never replace the wastebasket when it comes to streamlining office work. —*Clayton Elwell*

86. There is nothing more miserable in the world than to arrive in paradise and look like your passport photo. —*Erma Bombeck*

87. The trouble with most of us is that we would rather be ruined by praise than saved by criticism. —*Norman Vincent Peale*

88. Another flaw in the human character is that everybody wants to build and nobody wants to do maintenance. —*Kurt Vonnegut*

89. The depressing thing about tennis is that no matter how good I get, I'll never be as good as a wall. —*Mitch Hedberg*

90. We may not return the affection of those who like us, but we always respect their good judgment. —*Libbie Fudim*

91. They should put expiration dates on clothes so we would know when they go out of style. —*Garry Shandling*

92. I went to a high school that was so dangerous, the school newspaper had an obituary column. —*Rocky Ray*

93. Self-discipline is when your conscience tells you to do something and you don't talk back. —*W.K. Hope*

94. Middle age is the awkward period when Father Time starts catching up with Mother Nature. —*Harold Coffin*

95. Irony is when you buy a suit with two pairs of pants, and then burn a hole in the coat. —*Laurence Peter*

96. A doctor's reputation is made by the number of eminent men who die under his care. —*George Bernard Shaw*

97. I figure when my husband comes home from work, if the kids are still alive, then I've done my job. —*Roseanne*

98. One has to look out for engineers—they begin with sewing machines and end up with the atomic bomb. —*Marcel Pagnol*

99. As a teenager, I was more of an anarchist, but now I want people to thrive and be harmonious. —*Nicolas Cage*

100. Oh dear, I never realized what a terrible lot of explaining one has to do in a murder! —*Agatha Christie*

101. I learned to put the toilet seat down. It makes you look like a warm, caring, sensitive human being. —*Ralph Noble*

102. Always be nice to those younger than you, because they are the ones who will be writing about you. —*Cyril Connolly*

103. A family vacation is one where you arrive with five bags, four kids and seven I-thought-you-packed-its. —*Ivern Ball*

104. The first sign of maturity is the discovery that the volume knob also turns to the left. —*Chicago Tribune*

105. You can't always go by expert opinion. A turkey, if you ask a turkey, should be stuffed with grasshoppers, grit and worms. —*Anonymous*

106. Marriage is like twirling a baton, turning handsprings, or eating chopsticks. It looks easy until you try it. —*Helen Rowland*

107. When you reach for the stars, you may not quite get one, but you won't come up with a handful of mud either. —*Leo Burnett*

108. A bore is a man who spends so much time talking about himself that you can't talk about yourself. —*Melville Landon*

109. Will the people in the cheaper seats clap your hands? All the rest of you, if you'll just rattle your jewelry. —*John Lennon*

110. I thought I'd begin by reading a poem by Shakespeare, but then I thought, why should I? He never reads any of mine. —*Spike Mulligan*

111. The older I grow, the less important the comma becomes. Let the reader catch his own breath. —*Elizabeth Clarkson Zwart*

112. Sometimes the best way to convince someone he is wrong is to let him have his way. —*Red O'Donnell*

113. Fiction is like a spider's web, attached ever so slightly perhaps, but still attached to life at all four corners. —*Virginia Woolf*

114. I moved to New York City for my health. I'm paranoid and New York was the only place where my fears were justified. —*Anita Weiss*

115. You never see a man walking down the street with a woman who has a little potbelly and a bald spot. —*Elayne Boosler*

116. My neighbor asked if he could use my lawnmower and I told him of course he could, so long as he didn't take it out of my garden. —*Eric Morecambe*

117. Two of the hardest words in the English language to rhyme are life and love—of all words. —*Stephen Sondheim*

118. Whenever I hear anyone arguing for slavery, I feel a strong impulse to see it tried on him personally. *—Abraham Lincoln*

119. The real danger is not that computers will begin to think like men, but that men will begin to think like computers. *—Sydney Harris*

120. What my mother believed about cooking is that if you worked hard and prospered, someone else would do it for you. *—Nora Ephron*

121. Age does not depend upon years, but upon temperament and health. Some men are born old, and some never grow so. *—Tryon Edwards*

122. A doctor can bury his mistakes, but an architect can only advise his client to plant vines. *—Frank Lloyd Wright*

123. It was going all wrong at my college interview until I nonchalantly asked, "Do you need any large donations for new buildings?" *—Todd Anderson*

124. It is seldom that one parts on good terms, because if one were on good terms one would not part. *—Marcel Proust*

125. My doctor gave me six months to live, but when I couldn't pay the bill he gave me six months more. *—Walter Matthau*

126. There's one thing about children—they never go around showing snapshots of their grandparents. *—Bessie & Beulah*

127. Tact is the rare ability to keep silent while two friends are arguing, and you know both of them are wrong. *—Hugh Allen*

128. Optimism is a cheerful frame of mind that enables a teakettle to sing though in hot water up to its nose. *—Harold Helfer*

129. Even overweight cats instinctively know the cardinal rule: when fat, arrange yourself in slim poses. *—John Weitz*

130. Common sense is the most evenly distributed quantity in the world. Everyone thinks he has enough. *—René Descartes*

131. The first time I went to an American restaurant, they asked, "How many are in your party?" I said, "Two Million." *—Yakov Smirnoff*

132. I have noticed that the people who are late are often so much jollier than the people who have to wait for them. *—E. V. Lucas*

133. Creativity is allowing oneself to make mistakes. Art is knowing which ones to keep. *—Scott Adams*

134. Writers have a rare power not given to anyone else; we can bore people long after we are dead. *—Sinclair Lewis*

135. Since I've become a central banker, I've learned to mumble with great coherence. *—Alan Greenspan*

136. People who have no weaknesses are terrible; there is no way of taking advantage of them. *—Anatole France*

137. The reason most people play golf is to wear clothes they would not be caught dead in otherwise. —*Roger Simon*

138. This is a free country. Folks have a right to send me letters, and I have a right not to read them. —*William Faulkner*

139. The key to everything is patience. You get the chicken by hatching the egg, not by smashing it. —*Arnold H. Glasow*

140. Speak when you are angry and you will make the best speech you will ever regret. —*Ambrose Bierce*

141. Life may have no meaning. Or even worse, it may have a meaning of which I disapprove. —*Ashleigh Brilliant*

142. When people ask me if I have any spare change, I tell them I have it at home in my spare wallet. —*Nick Arnette*

143. I'll give you an idea of what kind of guy he was. Saint Francis would have punched him in the mouth. —*Gene Perret*

144. No man will make a great leader who wants to do it all himself or get all the credit for doing it. —*Andrew Carnegie*

145. For weeks I've been telling him not to buy anything for my birthday, and he still forgot to bring me something. —*Tanya Noe*

146. Use a make-up table with everything close at hand and don't rush; otherwise you'll look like a patchwork quilt. —*Lucille Ball*

147. For some reason, a lot of Hollywood big shots are curious to see how they'd be drawn with bulging eyes and no chin. —*Matt Groening*

148. There are no innocent bystanders. What were they doing there in the first place? —*William S. Burroughs*

149. I wish there was a knob on the TV to turn up the intelligence. There's a knob called "brightness," but it doesn't work. —*Gallagher*

150. Being a woman is a terribly difficult trade, since it consists principally of dealing with men. —*Joseph Conrad*

151. A dog teaches a boy fidelity, perseverance, and to turn around three times before lying down. —*Robert Benchley*

152. By working faithfully eight hours a day, you may eventually get to be a boss and work twelve hours a day. —*Robert Frost*

153. The reformer does not understand that people would rather be wrong and comfortable than right in jail. —*Finley Peter Dunne*

154. Adam invented love at first sight, one of the greatest labor-saving machines the world ever saw. —*Josh Billings*

155. There are more men than women in mental hospitals—which just goes to show who's driving who crazy. —*Peter Veale*

156. The really frightening thing about middle age is the knowledge that you'll grow out of it. —*Doris Day*

157. My movies are the kind they show in prisons and on airplanes because nobody can leave. —*Burt Reynolds*

158. Perseverance is the hard work you do after you get tired of doing the hard word you already did. —*Newt Gingrich*

159. The reason grandparents and grandchildren get along so well is that they have a common enemy. —*Sam Levenson*

160. You've got to be very careful if you don't know where you're going, because you might not get there. —*Yogi Berra*

161. An expert is a man who has made all the mistakes which can be made in a very narrow field. —*Niels Bohr*

162. I make a lot of money, but I don't want to talk about that. I work very hard and I'm worth every cent. —*Naomi Campbell*

163. My wife never lies about her age. She just tells everyone she's as old as I am. Then she lies about my age. —*Robert Orben*

164. The second day of a diet is always easier than the first. By the second day you're off it. —*Jackie Gleason*

165. It's discouraging to think how many people are shocked by honesty, and how few by deceit. —*Noel Coward*

166. The trouble with living life in the fast lane is that you get to the other end in an awful hurry. —*John Jensen*

167. An author who speaks about his own books is almost as bad as a mother who talks about her own children. —*Benjamin Disraeli*

168. As I usually do when I want to get rid of someone whose conversation bores me, I pretend to agree. —*Albert Camus*

169. Non-cooks think it's silly to invest two hours' work in two minutes' enjoyment; but if cooking is evanescent, so is the ballet. —*Julia Child*

170. The best measure of a man's honesty isn't his income tax return. It's the zero adjust on his bathroom scale. —*Arthur C. Clarke*

171. Long experience has taught me that in England nobody goes to the theater unless he or she has bronchitis. —*James Agate*

172. Being president is like running a cemetery; you've got a lot of people under you and nobody's listening. —*Bill Clinton*

173. They say wild animals only attack when they're cornered. I suppose that's why my goldfish was so calm when I flushed him.

—*Will Gillespie*

174. Whatever women must do they must do twice as well as men to be thought half as good. Luckily, this is not difficult. —*Charlotte Whitton*

175. I should not talk so much about myself if there were anybody else whom I knew as well. —*Henry David Thoreau*

176. The thing with pretending you're in a good mood is that sometimes you can actually trick yourself into feeling better.   *—Charles de Lint*

177. I am determined my children be brought up in their father's religion, if they can find out what it is.   *—Charles Lamb*

178. Work is the greatest thing in the world. So we should save some of it for tomorrow.   *—Don Herold*

179. I was on a date recently, and the guy took me horseback riding. That was kind of fun, until we ran out of quarters.   *—Susie Loucks*

180. A positive attitude will not solve all your problems, but it will annoy enough people to make it worth the effort.   *—Herm Albright*

181. The ultimate goal of the educational system is to shift to the individual the burden of pursuing his education.   *—John Gardner*

182. When they call the roll in the Senate, the Senators do not know whether to answer "Present" or "Not Guilty."   *—Theodore Roosevelt*

183. Proposed simplified tax form: How much money did you make last year? Mail it in.   *—Stanton Delaplane*

184. I'm all in favor of keeping dangerous weapons out of the hands of fools. Let's start with typewriters.   *—Solomon Short*

185. A healthy male adult bore consumes each year one and a half times his own weight in other people's patience.   *—John Updike*

186. Every man has a right to utter what he thinks truth, and every other man has a right to knock him down for it.   *—Samuel Johnson*

187. The future, according to some scientists, will be exactly like the past, only far more expensive.   *—John Thomas Sladek*

188. The reason why so few good books are written is that so few people who can write know anything.   *—Walter Bagehot*

189. If you want your children to improve, let them overhear the nice things you say about them to others.   *—Haim Ginott*

190. Never worry about the size of your Christmas tree. In the eyes of children, they are all thirty feet tall.   *—Larry Wilde*

191. Women and cats will do as they please, and men and dogs should relax and get used to the idea.   *—Robert A. Heinlein*

192. Old age is like a plane flying through a storm. Once you're aboard, there's nothing you can do about it.   *—Golda Meir*

193. Criticism, like rain, should be gentle enough to nourish a man's growth without destroying his roots.   *—Frank A. Clark*

194. Technology is a way of organizing the universe so that man doesn't have to experience it.   *—Max Frisch*

195. Married life teaches one invaluable lesson: to think of things far enough ahead not to say them.   *—Jefferson Machamer*

196. If only one could tell true love from false love as one can tell mushrooms from toadstools. —*Katharine Mansfield*

197. Technological progress has merely provided us with more efficient means for going backwards. —*Aldous Huxley*

198. Growing old is like being increasingly penalized for a crime you haven't committed. —*Anthony Powell*

199. If life were just, we would be born old and achieve youth about the time we'd saved enough to enjoy it. —*Jim Fiebig*

200. Instant availability without constant presence is probably the best role a mother can play. —*Lotte Bailyn*

201. Behold the turtle: he only makes success when he sticks his neck out. —*James Bryant Conant*

202. Man does not live by words alone, despite the fact that sometimes he has to eat them. —*Adlai Stevenson*

203. Politicians who complain about the media are like sailors who complain about the sea. —*Enoch Powell*

204. I am not a vegetarian because I love animals; I am a vegetarian because I hate plants. —*A. Whitney Brown*

205. Money can't buy you happiness, but it can buy you a yacht big enough to pull up right alongside it. —*David Lee Roth*

206. All marriages are happy. It's trying to live together afterwards that causes all the problems. —*Shelley Winters*

207. He that has no fools, knaves nor beggars in his family was begot by a flash of lightning. —*Thomas Fuller*

208. Hollywood is a place where they place you under contract instead of under observation. —*Walter Winchell*

209. I have discovered that all human evil comes from this: man's being unable to sit still in a room. —*Blaise Pascal*

210. Correct me if I'm wrong, but hasn't the fine line between sanity and madness gotten finer? —*George Price*

211. Do not condemn the judgment of another because it differs from your own. You may both be wrong. —*Dandemis*

212. Tact is the art of making guests feel at home when that's really where you wish they were. —*George E. Bergman*

213. If there's anyone listening to whom I owe money, I'm prepared to forget it if you are. —*Errol Flynn*

214. The better we feel about ourselves, the fewer times we have to knock somebody else down to feel tall. —*Odetta*

215. If you treat every situation as a life-and-death matter, you'll die a lot of times. —*Dean Smith*

216. If moral behavior were simply following rules, we could program a computer to be moral. —*Samuel P. Ginder*

217. There must be something to acupuncture—after all, you never see any sick porcupines. —*Bob Goddard*

218. Before most people start boasting about their family tree, they usually do a good pruning job. —*O.A. Battista*

219. Nobody will ever win the battle of the sexes. There's too much fraternizing with the enemy. —*Henry Kissinger*

220. Just when you think you've graduated from the school of experience, someone thinks up a new course. —*Mary H. Waldrip*

221. Sometimes a person has to go a very long distance out of his way to come back a short distance correctly. —*Edward Albee*

222. I have discovered the art of deceiving diplomats. I tell them the truth and they never believe me. —*Camillo di Cavour*

223. It took me seventeen years to get three thousand hits in baseball. I did it in one afternoon on the golf course. —*Hank Aaron*

224. You may think it's a long way down the road to the drug store, but that's just peanuts to space. —*Douglas Adams*

225. People who make history know nothing about history. You can see that in the sort of history they make. —*G.K. Chesterton*

226. Before I got married, I had six theories about bringing up children; now I have six children and no theories. —*John Wilmot*

227. A man who views the world the same at fifty as he did at twenty has wasted thirty years of his life. —*Muhammad Ali*

228. In a better-ordered world, the gypsy moth would show up in October and eat the leaves after they've fallen. —*Edward Stevenson*

229. Men occasionally stumble on the truth, but most of them pick themselves up and hurry off as if nothing had happened. —*Winston Churchill*

230. Conversation, which is supposed to be a two-way street, is treated by many as if it were a divided highway. —*Miss Manners*

231. Children have never been very good at listening to their elders, but they have never failed to imitate them. —*James Baldwin*

232. Death is a very dull, dreary affair, and my advice to you is to have nothing whatever to do with it. —*W. Somerset Maugham*

233. We pride ourselves on our ability to get a pizza to our door faster than an ambulance. —*Will Durst*

234. I sometimes wonder if the manufacturers of foolproof items keep a fool or two on their payroll to test things. —*Alan Coren*

235. My advice to you is get married: if you find a good wife you'll be happy; if not, you will become a philosopher. —*Socrates*

236. If some great catastrophe is not announced every morning, we feel a certain void. Nothing in the paper today, we sigh. —*Lord Acton*

237. You must get involved to have an impact. No one is impressed with the won-lost record of the referee. —*John H. Holcomb*

238. It is a great help for a man to be in love with himself. For an actor, however, it is absolutely essential. —*Robert Morley*

239. There are three stages of man: he believes in Santa Claus, he does not believe in Santa Claus, he is Santa Claus. —*Bob Phillips*

240. The trouble with telling a good story is that it invariably reminds the other fellow of a dull one. —*Sid Caesar*

241. Getting an idea should be like sitting on a pin. It should make you jump up and do something. —*E.L. Simpson*

242. Do not worry about your problems with mathematics; I assure you mine are far greater. —*Albert Einstein*

243. It is often hard to distinguish between the knocks of life and those of opportunity. —*Frederick Phillips*

244. Opportunity is missed by most people because it is dressed in overalls and looks like work. —*Thomas Edison*

245. The only thing that continues to give us more for our money is the weighing machine. —*George Clark*

246. Love, friendship, respect do not unite people as much as a common hatred for something. —*Anton Chekhov*

247. The worst moment for an atheist is when he feels grateful and has no one to thank. —*Wendy Ward*

248. In politics, if you want anything said, ask a man; if you want anything done, ask a woman. —*Margaret Thatcher*

249. The closest to perfection a person ever comes is when he fills out a job application form. —*Stanley J. Randall*

250. My doctor told me to stop having intimate dinners for four. Unless there are three other people. —*Orson Welles*

251. It's a recession when your neighbor loses his job; it's a depression when you lose your own. —*Harry S. Truman*

252. A great many people think they are thinking when they are merely rearranging their prejudices. —*William James*

253. A woman is like a tea bag—you can't tell how strong she is until you put her in hot water. —*Nancy Reagan*

254. Bankruptcy stared me in the face, but one thought kept me calm; soon I'd be too poor to need an anti-theft alarm. —*Gina Rothfels*

255. I loathe people who keep dogs. They are cowards who haven't got the guts to bite people themselves. —*August Strindberg*

256. I find television very educating. Every time somebody turns on the set, I go into the other room and read a book. —*Groucho Marx*

257. Some couples divorce because of a misunderstanding; others, because they understand each other too well. —*Evan Esar*

258. There is only one difference between a madman and me. The madman thinks he is sane. I know I am mad. —*Salvador Dali*

259. Congress is continually appointing fact-finding committees, when what we really need are some fact-facing committees. —*Roger Allen*

260. Writing is the only profession where no one considers you ridiculous if you earn no money. —*Jules Renard*

261. Asking an incumbent member of Congress to vote for term limits is like asking a chicken to vote for Colonel Sanders. —*Bob Inglis*

262. If you think dogs can't count, try putting three dog biscuits in your pocket and then giving Fido only two of them. —*Phil Pastoret*

263. I won't say ours was a tough school, but we had our own coroner. We used to write essays like "What I'm Going to Be If I Grow Up." —*Lenny Bruce*

264. Dreaming permits each and every one of us to be quietly and safely insane every night of our lives. —*William Dement*

265. It is great to be a blonde. With low expectations it's very easy to surprise people. —*Pamela Anderson*

266. The two leading recipes for success are building a better mousetrap and finding a bigger loophole. —*Edgar A. Schoaff*

267. Middle age is having a choice between two temptations and choosing the one that'll get you home earlier. —*Dan Bennett*

268. If people really liked to work, we'd still be plowing the land with sticks and transporting goods on our backs. —*William Feather*

269. Human beings are the only creatures on earth that allow their children to come back home. —*Bill Cosby*

270. I don't care what you say about me, as long as you say something about me, and as long as you spell my name right. —*George M. Cohan*

271. One rule of action more important than all others consists in never doing anything that someone else can do for you. —*Calvin Coolidge*

272. I don't kill flies but I like to mess with their minds. I hold them above globes. They freak out and yell, "Whoa, I'm way too high!" —*Bruce Baum*

273. The beauty of having a low income is that there is not enough money to buy what you don't really need. —*Ray Inman*

274. Sixty minutes of thinking of any kind is bound to lead to confusion and unhappiness. —*James Thurber*

275. There's nothing wrong with Southern California that a rise in the ocean level wouldn't cure. —*Ross Macdonald*

276. I'm strangely proud of the wrinkles I have. What I'm giving up in elasticity, I'm gaining in wisdom. —*Suzanne Somers*

277. What people do behind closed doors is certainly not my concern unless I'm behind there with 'em. —*Dolly Parton*

278. Marriage is like a violin. After the beautiful music is over, the strings are still attached. —*Jacob Braude*

279. He looked as if he had been poured into his clothes and had forgotten to say "when." —*P.G. Wodehouse*

280. I've never been jealous. Not even when my dad finished the fifth grade a year before I did. —*Jeff Foxworthy*

281. One question: if this is the information age, how come nobody knows anything? —*Robert Mankoff*

282. The right to be heard does not automatically include the right to be taken seriously. —*Hubert H. Humphrey*

283. Three o'clock is always too late or too early for anything you want to do. —*Jean-Paul Sartre*

284. Blessed is the man who, having nothing to say, abstains from giving wordy evidence of the fact. —*George Eliot*

285. The remarkable thing about Shakespeare is that he really is very good, in spite of all the people who say he is very good. —*Robert Graves*

286. My wife has a slight impediment in her speech. Every now and then she stops to breathe. —*Jimmy Durante*

287. There's only one way to have a happy marriage and as soon as I learn what it is I'll get married again. —*Clint Eastwood*

288. In science, the credit goes to the man who convinces the world, not to whom the idea first occurs. —*Sir Francis Darwin*

289. There exists no politician in India daring enough to attempt to explain to the masses that cows can be eaten. —*Indira Gandhi*

290. A friendship between reporter and source lasts only until it is profitable for one to betray the other. —*Maureen Dowd*

291. Politicians are people who, when they see light at the end of the tunnel, go out and buy some more tunnel. —*John Quinton*

292. Politicians are the same all over. They promise to build a bridge even where there is no river. —*Nikita Khrushchev*

293. It is not worth an intelligent man's time to be in the majority. By definition, there are already enough people to do that. —*G.H. Hardy*

294. Justice is the insurance we have on our lives, and obedience is the premium we pay for it.
—*William Penn*

295. It is a dangerous thing for a national candidate to say things that people might remember.
—*Eugene McCarthy*

296. As one cat said to another: Birthdays are like fur balls—the more you have, the more you gag.
—*Marla Morgan*

297. Good communication is as stimulating as black coffee, and just as hard to sleep after.
—*Anne Morrow Lindbergh*

298. I believe Ronald Reagan can make this country what it once was ... a large arctic region covered with ice.
—*Steve Martin*

299. The great thing about democracy is that it gives every voter a chance to do something stupid.
—*Art Spander*

300. Going through life with a conscience is like driving your car with the brakes on.
—*Budd Schulberg*

301. Autobiography is an unrivaled vehicle for telling the truth about other people.
—*Philip Guedalla*

302. You know you are growing old when almost everything hurts, and what does not hurt does not work.
—*Hy Gardner*

303. Give your brain as much attention as you do your hair, and you'll be a thousand times better off.
—*Malcolm X*

304. If killing was the answer, we'd have solved all our problems a long time ago.
—*Dick Gregory*

305. Society is like a stew. If you don't keep it stirred up, you get a lot of scum on top.
—*Edward Abbey*

306. Nouvelle Cuisine, roughly translated, means: I can't believe I paid ninety-six dollars and I'm still hungry.
—*Mike Kalin*

307. There are only two classes of pedestrians in these days of reckless motor traffic—the quick and the dead.
—*Thomas Robert Dewar*

308. He had occasional flashes of silence that made his conversation perfectly delightful.
—*Sydney Smith*

309. I can't speak for any other marriage, but the secret of our marriage is that we have absolutely nothing in common.
—*Mamie Eisenhower*

310. One of the lessons of history is that nothing is often a good thing to do and always a clever thing to say.
—*Will Durant*

311. A man occupied with public or other important business cannot, and need not, attend to spelling.
—*Napoleon Bonaparte*

312. My grandfather's a little forgetful, but he likes to give me advice. One day, he took me aside and left me there.
—*Ron Richards*

313. The purpose of a liberal education is to make you philosophical enough to accept the fact that you will never make much money.
—*Norman Douglas*

314. If it's a bill, the post office will get it to you in twenty-four hours. If it's a check, allow them a couple weeks. —*Richard Needham*

315. A statistician is someone who is good at figures but who doesn't have the personality to be an accountant. —*Roy Hyde*

316. Home is a place you grow up wanting to leave, and grow old wanting to get back to. —*John Ed Pierce*

317. In order to make an apple pie from scratch, you must first create the universe. —*Carl Sagan*

318. The sports page records people's accomplishments, the front page nothing but their failures. —*Justice Earl Warren*

319. Some couples go over their budgets very carefully every month; others just go over them. —*Sally Poplin*

320. Buying stock is exactly the same thing as going to a casino, only with no cocktail service. —*Ted Allen*

321. The only person who listens to both sides of an argument is the fellow in the next apartment. —*Ruth Brown*

322. Nothing is so embarrassing as watching someone do something that you said couldn't be done. —*Sam Ewing*

323. If it weren't for electricity we'd all be watching television by candlelight. —*George Gobel*

324. He pasted picture postcards around goldfish bowls to make the goldfish think they were going places. —*Fred Allen*

325. I still say a church steeple with a lightning rod on top shows a lack of confidence. —*Doug MacLeod*

326. Being in the Army is like being in the Boy Scouts, except that the Boy Scouts have adult supervision. —*Blake Clark*

327. A study of economics usually reveals that the best time to buy anything is last year. —*Marty Allen*

328. I would never read a book if it were possible for me to talk half an hour with the man who wrote it. —*Woodrow Wilson*

329. It's hard for the modern generation to understand Thoreau, who lived beside a pond but didn't own water skis or a snorkel.
—*Bill Vaughan*

330. English is a funny language. That explains why we park our car on the driveway and drive our car on the parkway. —*Mark Grasso*

331. Juries scare me. I don't want to put my faith in people who weren't smart enough to get out of jury duty. —*Monica Piper*

332. There is no point at which you can say, "Well, I'm successful now. I might as well take a nap." —*Carrie Fisher*

333. The reason there are so few female politicians is that it is too much trouble to put make-up on two faces. —*Maureen Murphy*

334. A satirist is a man who discovers unpleasant things about himself and then says them about other people. —*Peter McArthur*

335. Ninety-nine percent of the people in the world are fools, and the rest of us are in great danger of contagion. —*Thornton Wilder*

336. The importance of a public speaker bears an inverse relationship to the number of microphones into which he speaks. —*William Morgan*

337. It's not that I write well, I just don't write badly very often, and that passes for good on television. —*Andy Rooney*

338. The U.S. is the only country where failure to promote yourself is widely considered arrogant. —*Garry Trudeau*

339. We owe to the Middle Ages the worst two inventions of humanity— romantic love and gun powder. —*Andre Maurois*

340. I'm absolutely sure there is no life on Mars. It's not listed on my daughter's phone bill. —*Larry Matthews*

341. Any event, once it has occurred, can be made to appear inevitable by a competent historian. —*Lee Simonson*

342. My first wife divorced me on the grounds of incompatibility, and besides I think she hated me. —*Oscar Levant*

343. A highbrow is the kind of person who looks at a sausage and thinks of Picasso. —*Alan Patrick Herbert*

344. What is my loftiest ambition? I've always wanted to throw an egg into an electric fan. —*Oliver Herford*

345. If you ever see me getting beaten by the police, put down the video camera and come help me. —*Bobcat Goldthwait*

346. He's turned his life around. He used to be miserable and depressed, now he's depressed and miserable. —*David Frost*

347. There are some ideas so wrong that only a very intelligent person could believe them. —*George Orwell*

348. Want to have some fun? Send someone a telegram saying, "Ignore first telegram." —*Henny Youngman*

349. Abstract art: a product of the untalented sold by the unprincipled to the utterly bewildered. —*Al Capp*

350. I'm proud of paying taxes. The only thing is—I could be just as proud for half the money. —*Arthur Godfrey*

351. Why does a woman work ten years to change a man's habits and then complain that he's not the man she married? —*Barbra Streisand*

352. Yesterday I was a dog. Today I'm a dog. Tomorrow I'll probably still be a dog. Sigh! There's so little hope for advancement. —*Snoopy*

353. Business is never so healthy as when, like a chicken, it must do a certain amount of scratching for what it gets. —*Henry Ford*

354. One difference between death and taxes is that death doesn't get worse every time Congress meets. —*Roy Schaefer*

355. In a few minutes a computer can make a mistake so great that it would take many men many months to equal it. —*Merle. L. Meacham*

356. I would rather that the people wonder why I wasn't President than why I am. —*Salmon P. Chase*

357. When a man retires and time is no longer of urgent importance, his colleagues generally present him with a watch. —*R.C. Sherriff*

358. What a pity human beings can't exchange problems. Everyone knows exactly how to solve the other fellow's. —*Olin Miller*

359. If you don't mind smelling like peanut butter for two or three days, peanut butter is darn good shaving cream. —*Barry Goldwater*

360. What lucky thing that the wheel was invented before the automobile; otherwise, can you imagine the awful screeching? —*Samuel Hoffenstein*

361. I'm a godmother. That's a great thing to be, a godmother. She calls me god for short. That's cute. I taught her that. —*Ellen DeGeneres*

362. You know when you're young, you think your dad's Superman. Then you grow up and realize he's just a regular guy who wears a cape. —*Dave Atell*

363. It is well to remember that the entire universe, with one trifling exception, is composed of others. —*John Andrew Holmes*

364. It's just as sure a recipe for failure to have the right idea fifty years too soon as five years too late. —*J.R. Platt*

365. Football incorporates the two worst elements of American society: violence punctuated by committee meetings. —*George Will*

366. Education is a wonderful thing. If you couldn't sign your name you'd have to pay cash. —*Rita Mae Brown*

367. Today it takes more brains to fill out the income tax form than it does to make the income. —*Alfred E. Neuman*

368. Medicine, the only profession that labors incessantly to destroy the reason for its existence. —*James Bryce*

369. People always come up to me and say that my smoking is bothering them. Well it's killing me! —*Wendy Liebman*

370. I got the bill for my surgery. Now I know what those doctors were wearing masks for. —*James H. Boren*